How To Write A Book:

Writing A Novel That Sells

Dan Brown

NMD Books
Simi Valley, CA

Library of Congress Cataloging-in-Publication
How To Write A Book: Writing A Novel That Sells
by Dan Brown
ISBN:978-1-936828-44-9 (Softcover)

First Edition March 2016

CONTENTS

INTRODUCTION

I never knew any writers before I started to write. Until then I thought books and paintings and music just poured out of special people called "artists," who possessed a rare quality called "talent," which was easily recognized at a very early age and immutable, like the color of their eyes. These misconceptions led me to asking the wrong questions, like, "Am I good?" or "Am I too old to start?" They led me into agonies of fear and self-hate and paralysis every time I encountered the ordinary, daily problems in the process of writing. They led me to making resolutions to quit, followed by dejected crawling back to the typewriter because I couldn't quit.

After a while I quit quitting, gave up asking myself if I was a "real" writer, accepted my compulsion, and asked people to recommend books that would help me. Some teachers gave me titles of excellent books that were worse than no help at all. Written by critics examining the finished products of great masters, these books scared me by pointing out inimitable achievements, and, though they helped me to be a better reader, they told me nothing about the process of writing.

"No," I told my teachers, "I need something that will help me get started every morning." They laughed.

So I kept on writing. And I kept on searching for what other writers might have written about the process of writing. I found little help and most of it in scraps: a paragraph from an interview or letter or essay; sometimes even an anthology of scraps, like Walter Allen's *Writers on Writing.*

After twenty years of writing, I understand the laughter of my teachers, for I know we all still need something to help us get started every morning. In fact, as most experienced writers will tell you, it gets harder, perhaps because, as Mary Austin expressed it in her

Everyman's Genius, every new project requires, "... a new alignment of the various faculties of the self that produces it. So at the beginning of every piece of creative work there is almost always a time of struggle and torment for the producer." In other words, we are all perennial beginners.

Yet there are some things an experienced beginner can tell a new beginner, some misconceptions I can correct, some shocks I might spare you. That is what I have tried to do here, to answer some of the questions beginners ask, to write the kind of book I was searching for when I started.

I mention a few other useful books in passing. But I do not provide a recommended reading list because such a list would start with all the great and good novels, stories, plays and poems ever written. Those are the books from which we learn the most, and we do best to find our way through them at a rate and in an order which suits us individually.

When I can, I cite experience from writers I admire. More often I give examples from my own work, published and unpublished, because my own writing process is what I know best, most deeply, and first hand. This experience is offered with a disclaimer similar to the one Thoreau gave readers of his Walden, when he warned them not to look for him in the woods because by the time they got there he might be somewhere else. What I offer is not a set of rules but a picture of a working process still developing, a guide toward asking the right questions, the ones you eventually find answers for in yourself, in your work.

This book, then, contains nothing new. It only brings together parts of the process as I have experienced it and found it confirmed by most fiction writers, most of the time. What I tell you may mean little until you reach the same conclusions through your own work, but I hope I give hints that nudge you in the right direction, toward your own answers.

These hints are addressed to novelists but (excluding the planning section) may help in writing short stories too.

Finally, on the subject of getting published, all I can offer is this urgent suggestion: while you are fighting and waiting through the publishing struggle, start your next book.

2

Gathering the Material

1. The Seed

Henry James called it the seed or germ: an image, a glimpse of a person, shreds of overheard dialogue, a casual reference dropped in conversation at dinner by a woman sitting next to him. In his preface to *The Spoils of Poynton* James insisted that the seed must be small, rough, incomplete, that if the woman enlarged upon her anecdote, she would kill it. He could use only that hint, which he believed a writer instantly recognizes as his material.

But these hints are not always recognized. In Art and Reality Joyce Cary tells us he once wrote a story weeks after catching and forgetting a glimpse of a young woman on a ferry boat. The story was nearly finished before he realized that it had come out of that brief moment, or had been triggered by it.

It was Gary's good luck, or a sign of his development, that his raw material grabbed him in spite of himself. Some of our best ideas come as rather weak clicks in the mind, clicks that may be easily ignored in the general noise of living. The seed of Ella Price's journal was such a weak, frequently heard click that I had ignored it many times before I really heard it: a middle-aged woman sitting in my office at the college where I taught in the mid-sixties, crying and telling me that going to school was both saving her life and destroying it. Click. Here is the heroine of an invisible drama, heroine of a novel. Ever since that book was published teachers have been telling me they "kicked themselves" for not having written Ella's story, which they all knew so well. But that statement only shows their ignorance of the first step in writing fiction: to see what is so familiar to everyone that it has become invisible.

It is these little clicks, rather than the great flashes, that usually develop into a story. I have had great ideas for novels. They come down on me like fireworks, bursting with excitement, and may keep me in a state of sleepless euphoria for days. But I have learned to be suspicious of them because they so often turn out to be more intersting than anything I can do with them. Or, and this is somewhat embarrassing, they turn out, on close examination, to be mere spinoff from reading someone else's book. Not my fresh treatment of similar themes, but trite imitation. If you are seduced into such flashy imitation, you may have to go through a whole rough draft or even beyond before some sharp critic deflates your overblown creation. Months of exhilarating, inspired work, and then someone tells you it's trite. And, worst of all, you know he's right! What can be done about it? Just survive that stage. (Simple endurance is an essential part of "talent") Eventually, with more reading and writing, you spot a phony seed quickly and waste no time on it.

A surprising number of great novels have come from items in newspapers, not usually from the important political articles that responsible citizens read, but from the obscure, squalid, often violent stories on the back pages. Dreiser's American Tragedy and Stendhal's The Red and the Black came from news accounts of men killing their mistresses. Tolstoy's Anna Karenina and Flaubert's Madame Bovary both came from accounts of suicides, though in the case of Flaubert's seed, it was actually the husband who had killed himself, not the wife.

Flaubert's use of the seed brings up the question of the transformation that occurs as seed moves toward story. The seed is only the starting point; you are under no obligation to stick to "what really happened." If you read background material on Chekhov's play The Seagull, you'll be amused to find that the seed and model for the vulnerable and appealing Nina was actually a silly and boring woman who pursued Chekhov relentlessly, inflating a casual acquaintance to ludicrous melodrama. Somehow Chekhov transformed his impatience and her longings, dignified her soap opera fantasies and turned them into real pathos. Maybe we should call this the "pestasseed" principle and comfort ourselves with plans to use our own pests in a book someday.

Many seeds come out of our memory. The one for one of my own stories was a recollection which erupted in anger when a friend made a disparaging remark about "hatchet-faced old maid schoolteachers."

4

Suddenly I was defending a woman I saw clearly though I had never known her well and had not thought of her for twenty five years.

A seed can be cerebral. An intellectual game of "What if..." often leads to its seeming opposite, intuitive fantasy. The Kin of Ate Are Waiting For. You came to me while I was reading Jung and thought, what if people lived in obedience to their dreams?

Readers are disappointed when I tell them that. They want to hear that the whole book came to me in a dream. No novel ever comes that easily, but seeds might. Many writers find their dreams a rich source of seeds. (Dreams not only give us seeds but exemplify the process of turning seeds into stories. Writers often say writing fiction is like dreaming, where the actual and the imagined are woven together into a symbolic, sometimes even mythic statement.)

The novel I am working on now grew out of a glimpse of a young blind mother holding her baby and talking to her husband in a motel on the edge of Death Valley. The more I work on it, the further my story moves from that woman toward a story I have been waiting almost thirty years to tell, waiting for the right click to push me toward discovering it.

I have written one unpublished novel and several stories that came out of seeds of frustration, confusion, pain and rage, out of trying to understand my failure, utter failure, to cope with problems that confronted me. I didn't solve any problems by writing about them; fiction doesn't solve problems, it states them, which is harder to do than most people think. What I did was to use the writing to help me live through situations I could neither escape nor control. Further, I used my pain, probed it as material for a story, not only gaining insight into it, but coming out of the experience with something to show for it. This ability to use pain is the great advantage of writers which Somerset Mangham declares, in The Summing Up, makes all disadvantages of writing unimportant. "Nothing befalls him that he cannot transmute into a stanza, a song or a story, and having done this be rid of it. The artist is the only free man."

5

2. "Nothing important has ever happened to me"

I got that sentence out of a sad, repeated experience of my teaching days, and I put it into Ella Price's journal. Ella's teacher gives her a list of suggested topics for writing in her journal. When Ella reaches "important experience," she writes, "Nothing important has ever happened to me." That sentence had haunted me for years, turning up in dozens of journals handed in by students of all ages in my remedial composition classes. It seemed to me to be the key to their inability to write. Not only had they closed themselves to the richness and pain of their daily experience, but they had come to the point where they dismissed as "unimportant" their lives and, by implication, their very selves.

What does this story have to do with you? Nothing, I hope. If you see this section as an unnecessary interruption, introducing a problem you don't have, then you are happily free of a crippling inhibition.

However, I have observed that many beginning writers of fiction devalue their own experience. The egotistical bore who, this month, fancies herself a great writer, will pour out her every thought and act, certain that nothing in the world is more important. But the serious writer often begins tentatively, modestly, uncertainly. She may dismiss her own experience as inadequate, pulling out from under herself the base on which she must stand if she is to transcend the limitations of her experience by transforming it into art. And sometimes this self-destructive tendency is encouraged by the very people who ought to know better.

In the late fifties, when I was starting, there was a notion prevalent among writers that "real" life was observed only in bars, on ghetto streets, in brothels, and on battlefields. If this idea was hard on academic men, it was death on women writers, since a woman who tried to observe life from a bar stool or a slum street corner was usually interrupted by some drunken bore, if not by something worse. Battlefields were out, and working in a brothel seemed to me a bit further than I was willing to go for my art, notwithstanding Norman Mailer's announcement that there would be no great novels written by women until a call girl wrote her memoirs.

I cannot remember anyone pointing out to him that Jane Austen and the Bronte sisters did pretty well with almost unimaginably isolated and circumscribed lives. Compared to them, compared to Proust or, in fact, to most pre-twentieth century people, the writer today, of whatever sex, class or location, lives a life so full of experience that the main problem could be a surfeit of events so distracting as to make writing impossible. Even if you were locked up in a cell tomorrow and kept there alone for the rest of your life, you would have more material from memory and dreams than you could ever write about.

Anything can be material for a novel. The more ordinary, the more mundane, the more "unimportant" it seems, the more rich it may be, though no one else may think so while you are working on it, and you will have your own doubts. When I was trying to sell Ella Price's journal, the resistance of publishers was summed up by one editor who rejected it with a breezy, "Oh, of course, we all know women like your heroine, but they are not interesting enough to sustain a novel." Within four years interest had shifted, at least temporarily, toward women like my heroine. So don't judge the value of your seeds by salability or by what other people are thinking about; they may just be a few years behind you.

Don't judge your seeds by the fact that most of them refuse to grow into stories. Like the Biblical parable of the broadcast seeds, only a few of which fell on fertile soil, most seeds or clicks come to nothing. But that's all right because you only need one, the right one, for a couple of years of work.

And if you have even a scrap of that nothing important ever happened to me feeling, you must drive it out, perhaps by making a sign to hang over your desk and by constant repetition of a mantra made up of some phrases from William Blake, "... to see a world in a grain of sand ... for everything that lives is holy ..." or any other uncompromising assertion of the worth of all experience.

3. Catching Your Seeds

Novelists who have learned to listen to their clicks say that their subject chooses them and that they could not write any book other than

7

the one they are working on, no matter what more brilliant or more salable ideas other people press upon them. These writers have learned to maintain an alert passivity which leaves them open to being chosen by their material. The serious writer tries to maintain this open receptivity, day or night, awake or asleep, always ready to be chosen by the few special seeds (among the millions) that have his or her name on them.

Don't misunderstand me. I have no patience with people who say the artist must become a mere spectator, always detached, not really living but noting and setting down the passionate living of other, less conscious beings. As if our minds could only do one thing at a time! Feel or think. Do or watch. No, we must learn to fuse all artificially divided abilities to sense, feel, deduct, perceive, and conclude. To live and to understand. To care and to analyze. To be totally involved while being totally clear and objective. Impossible? Well, maybe, but I keep trying.

If you want to know more about the alert, receptive, involved yet objective state of mind in which you allow yourself to be chosen by women like your heroine, but they are not interesting enough to sustain a novel." Within four years interest had shifted, at least temporarily, toward women like my heroine. So don't judge the value of your seeds by salability or by what other people are thinking about; they may just be a few years behind you.

Don't judge your seeds by the fact that most of them refuse to grow into stories. Like the Biblical parable of the broadcast seeds, only a few of which fell on fertile soil, most seeds or clicks come to nothing. But that's all right because you only need one, the right one, for a couple of years of work.

And if you have even a scrap of that nothing important ever happened to me feeling, you must drive it out, perhaps by making a sign to hang over your desk and by constant repetition of a mantra made up of some phrases from William Blake, "... to see a world in a grain of sand ... for everything that lives is holy ..." or any other uncompromising assertion of the worth of all experience.

Are most of these names and titles unfamiliar to you? Not surprising. One of the great deprivations of the twentieth century is to be cut off (especially if you received a "good" college education) from the vast, deeply poetic, broadly psychological literature of the mystics, those people who know a Reality beyond what little we perceive through our five senses and who try to tell us about possibilities of the higher consciousness they have experienced and have dedicated their lives to exploring. (You experience a tiny hint of this consciousness when you thrill to great art or to awesome nature or to falling in love.)

Unfortunately there is no direct, precise vocabulary in any language to describe these experiences and their meaning. The symbols and rituals and myths of most religions evolved from attempts by mystics to describe their experiences, their methods of consciousness. Old rituals and myths lost meaning, religious institutions lost moral force, technology and intellect became objects of worship. The result was that a great literature was thrown out or relegated to the realm of fervently sentimental holy tracts ignored by people who consider themselves serious, educated and intelligent. A terrible loss to everyone but especially to artists, because so much of our work depends on a balance between our intuitive and rational powers, but must start with the intuitive, with "another way of knowing," as the mystics (including many artists) would say.

If you start reading mystical literature, chances are you will be turned off by the religious symbols. Don't just read the words; try to approach them freshly, as metaphors for developing creative powers. For instance, try reading "The Sermon on the Mount," not as a set of rules for flaccid capitulation to abuse and injustice, but as a manual for creative artists, a list of exercises for freeing yourself from the mean, petty obsessions, often referred to as the seven deadly sins, which get between you and what you can know wholly, and which steal from you the energy you need to transmute this knowledge into your work and your life. (On one level my The Kin of Ata Are Waiting for You is a manual of this type, tracing the stages of growing consciousness through which a fragmented man becomes a whole, serious artist.)

If you can rid yourself of prejudice and approach such "religious" writings freshly, you will be amazed at how they express and help strengthen your most profound need to open yourself to the possibilities of your talent. An aid in this fresh approach is Aldous Huxley's The Perennial Philosophy, an anthology of mystical writings

9

strung together with Huxley's commentary and followed by a fine bibliography.

We are, by the way, just coming out of a period when many people experimented with chemical shortcuts to open up their consciousness, with sometimes transiently interesting, and sometimes disastrous results. Drugs remain a tempting device, partly because they fit the old superstitions about the artist as madman, irrationally and outrageously "uninhibited" (meaning rude, irresponsible, drunken, ruthless and dirty). All of these traits are supposed, according to this belief, to have something to do with the periodic gushing out of inspired creative work, and I hate to think of how many creeps we have put up with, waiting for the creative product we thought would eventually come out of the mess they made. Some artists are creeps, to be sure, but no more than you'll find in the general population. Some artists use liquor and drugs, but seldom while working.

Drugs are also tempting because we are a nation of pill-takers, and although the person who says, "I need to take this to unleash my creativity," doesn't like to think so, he is acting in the tradition of all the people who live on Exlax and Valium. He is also confusing feeling creative with being creative.

If you're too tense to be easily receptive to seeds, liquor or drugs may take the edge off and make you more open. But while gaining receptivity, you may lose the faculties which organize, form, and complete a work of art. So if you're still in the early, often painful stages of opening up to experience, you'd be wise to start hunting for other relaxers: deep breathing, meditation, yoga, swimming, walking, laughing, praying. (The last two are the same, says the artist hero of Joyce Gary's novel *The Horse's Mouth.)*

4. "Write about what you know."(?)

I am willing to repeat that oldest rule for beginners, but please note that I add a question mark, which means this is a good idea that doesn't always apply.

I'll give you an example of a case in which it did apply. I once had a writing student who wrote endlessly detailed accounts of his early life, sometimes mildly interesting, but more often boring lists of incidents, raw material that seemed somehow flat. He wanted to write a novel, but he could not let himself play with this material, changing these experiences, selecting, shaping them as fiction. He could not let himself deviate from telling "what really happened," and when I quoted Picasso's, "The artist lies in order to tell the truth," he looked at me suspiciously. Furthermore it was clear to me that in writing "what really happened" he was selecting safe, smooth parts of his life, not the ones that haunt our dreams, not the ones that, as Chekhov said, make us feel we're writing the story in our own blood. (Chekhov also said we shouldn't bother to write unless we felt like that.) When I hinted that he might be censoring some of the material, I only made him more defensive. And when I suggested that he loosen up by writing, in literal detail, some of his dreams, he looked shocked.

Then one day he came to me, glowing triumphantly, and handed me the first chapter of a novel. The setting for this novel was an Asian battlefield, the hero was a physician, the action on sea and land was full of violence, and all the other characters were "hard-bitten" soldiers. This from a writer with no combat experience, no medical training.

Yet every word of it was instantly recognizable, and since we cannot write without revealing ourselves, he had revealed his television, movie and (sparse) reading habits. He had also revealed the class insecurities which contributed to his inhibition, his rejecting or banalizing of material from his own life: in making the hero a "doctor" he had copied the portrait of the all-knowing soap opera doctor, the stereotype concocted to be viewed by poor people who have no intimate knowledge of people in the "professions" but who accept them as heroes because they cannot respect their own lives, their own heroism, as material worth turning into art. As you can imagine, the style of this piece of work matched the material (not raw, but artificial, processed and overcooked) he had used.

What could I tell him? Any direct appraisal would have humiliated him and would have sounded like arrogant amateur psychoanalysis, anticipating things he would have to learn and learn to deal with when he was ready.

With seeming irrelevance I mentioned a book. Jack London's Martin Eden, which I said he might enjoy. I hoped he'd read the novel

11

and get indirect support from it, as I once had in my struggle as a lower class beginner. (If he had been of a different background and temperament, I'd have suggested some other novel about an artist: Willa Gather's *Song of the Lark,* James Joyce's *Portrait of the Artist as a Young Man,* May Sarton's *Mrs. Stevens Hears the Mermaids Singing,* Samuel Butler's *The Way of All Flesh,* Joyce Gary's *The Horse's Mouth,* Ralph Ellison's *Invisible Man.*)

Then I congratulated him on breaking out of his fear of invention, in going beyond the recital of literal event following event. "But," I said as gently as I could, "this is not really your subject," and urged him to apply this new freedom to situations and people he knew well. "Write about what you know."

Offended, doubting my judgment and taste (Wasn't his chapter every bit as good as what TV writers were paid for? Yes it was, but... he argued with me for a few minutes and then left. He never came back, so I don't know whether he later changed his mind and, like most writers, came to view this early effort with amusement.

5. Know about what you write.

But the injunction to write about what you know must not become a strangle hold on the imagination. After all, you can usually find out about what you don't know. Stephen Crane also wrote about battles he had never fought or seen, wrote with no combat experience at all, but he talked with men who had before he wrote *The Red Badge of Courage.* And although Civil War veterans complained that Crane got some of his facts wrong, their complaints became irrelevant as readers realized the deeper truths of this classic which became a new model for men in battle novels.

In his essay "The Art of Fiction" Henry James assures us that a very little experience or observation goes a long way for the writer who has developed the "power to guess the unseen from the seen." We make such guesses all the time. You can catch a look or word between a man and woman and know it means he is still in love while she is getting bored, and you can imagine and create all the authentic scenes leading up to and away from that look or word. Or you can reach out to pet a dog, see it cringe, know it has been mistreated and discover a whole new side which rounds out your portrait of its master. Women have always used this power in personal relationships, extrapolating from small signs, gestures, unconscious signals, more than men have. In women who don't write, this process is referred to as women's intuition. In writers of both sexes it is called talent. And it is, like all powers, developed by being used.

There is no subject which you should feel is beyond you if you are drawn to it, intrigued, if you think it is your seed. A man can write about a woman in childbirth. A woman can write a story set in a male army barracks. An adult can write from the point of view of a child, a middleclass black from the point of view of a poor white, and so on. Only three things are necessary. First, objective observation, as much as is possible. Second, the imagination to expand, to create "the unseen from the seen." Third, dipping down into that deep part of yourself where you are like all other human beings, feeling as they feel, knowing as they know, living their story as you write it.

After you have used these three processes to the best of your ability, you can show your work to a person knowledgeable in the "foreign" field you have invaded. This person can check your mistakes like the "technical directors" in movies who make sure there are no clocks in a film set in ancient Rome (though Shakespeare didn't worry about literal authenticity and in *Julius Caesar* everyone is always checking a "clock" for the time.).

Just make sure your "technical director" doesn't have problems of his own. A friend who read my *Kin of Ata* shook his head and pronounced it, "Not as subtle as your other work," the sort of comment so sure to crush me that I couldn't bear to ask him to explain. I should have. A couple of years later I heard him praising the book and reminded him of what he had said earlier. He blushed, shrugged, and said, "Well, I couldn't handle the fact that you had done a male point of view so well."

In creating fantasy, science fiction or historical novels, you must write from beyond any daily, literal experience or memory, creating worlds you never saw. In these cases, what Joseph Conrad said about all novels still applies: you must create a world in which you "can honestly believe," yet in some way "familiar to the experience. . .of. . . readers." That means researching the historical or scientific, or imagining the fantasy world of your novel, knowing it thoroughly as a consistent world. (More about this in the section on planning.) And it means your creatures and their story must connect symbolically with contemporary people and concerns.

In her biography of Charlotte Bronte, Elizabeth Gaskell gives this description of how Bronte approached writing about things she had not experienced:

"She had thought intently on it for many and many a night before falling to sleep,—wondering what it was like, or how it would be,—till at length, sometimes after the progress of her story had been arrested at this one point for weeks, she wakened up in the morning with all clear before her, as if she had in reality gone through the experience, and then could describe it, word for word, as it happened. I cannot account for this psychologically; I only am sure that it was so, because she said it."

I'm not contradicting everything I said about knowing about what you write or writing about what you know. But I must tell you, if you don't already know it, that we all try something like Bronte's intuitive or extrasensory reach of the imagination. And—sometime'—it works. These powers may be weak in us in comparison to Bronte. But they exist in all human beings, and they become highly developed in writers who have the courage and the stamina to exercise them.

6. Keep a journal.

Samuel Butler said the mark of a writer was the small notebook carried everywhere.

Hemingway said he never bothered to keep a journal because if an idea was worth using he wouldn't forget it.

I must concede to Hemingway that I have hardly ever glanced at my journals and have never searched them to find an idea for a book. Nevertheless I side with Butler because I know that the pile of dusty old composition books on my closet shelf is essential and must continue to grow. I seldom go more than a few days without writing in my journal, which I started even before I knew I was a writer. . . and which helped me find out that I am. I no longer carry my journal with me like a talisman, as I did in the beginning when I was finding this out. But I do carry a few 3x5 cards when I leave home, enough to scribble a note. Later, when I get home, I paste a scribbled card in my journal.

What should you write in your journal? Well. . .everything. You can start with your stomach ache or your lover's blindness to your needs or your inability to write. Virginia Woolf was rather apologetic about her diaries because in her later years she tended to write in them mostly when she was stuck on a book and feeling miserable, so they are full of fears and complaints, not presenting a true picture of her usual state of mind. Most writers, however, find these parts of her diaries rather reassuring, telling us that she too suffered from insecurities about her work, from tremendous fear of critics, and she too sometimes used her diaries as a kind of garbage dump. (Pretty special garbage, hers!)

Every journal contains a lot of garbage dump writing along with straight observation and narration. Does any of the garbage writing contain seeds? Sometimes. More often it is just junk that must be poured out to get you clear for collecting seeds. Where are the seeds? Well, again, everywhere, in everything. "Everything" can be an empty answer for beginners, so I will start a list of suggestions for you:

Suggested Journal Entries
1. description of an object, natural or manufactured
2. description of a person
3. description of an action
4. an interesting word or phrase
5. overheard conversation
6. a passage copied from another writer
7. an impromtu poem
8. a painful experience or memory
9. a strong emotion—tell what brought it on
10. word association—keep stringing out words until you run dry
11. a new word—define it and use it
12. ideas for stories, set off by objects or people or memory
13. anecdotes told by other people
14. an argument—what was it really about?
15. dreams

15

16. unusual visual effects
17. description of a room
18. incidents from memory
19. descriptions of animals
20. criticisms of stories, poems, films
21. letters or notes received in the mail
22. notices found on bulletin boards
23. evocative newspaper reports
24. interesting want ads
25. word invention
26. description of physical signs of strong emotional state
27. daydreams
28. ?
29. ?

It's not a bad list, if you see it as a beginning, a list you could add to forever. If you're just starting to keep a journal, you may want to copy this list on the first page, with additions, and with Henry James' admonition, "Try to be one of the people on whom nothing is lost!"

The journal or notebook or diary has many uses. Some writers go back to entries written years ago and suddenly see the story possibilities, or find the one necessary element that fits the book they're writing. Even if you're like me and hardly ever glance again at what you've written in your journal, the act of writing it down does something. I once knew a teacher of study skills who told his students to write a brief outline or summary of each chapter they were studying for a test. Students who followed his advice reported that, without looking again at their summaries, they easily passed the test. The act of writing something captures it in some more secure spot of the mind, stops up the holes through which so many of our ideas and observations leak out. So, whether or not you reread your journals, you use them as safe storage for seeds. And storage is part of the process. I can't remember ever starting a novel immediately after collecting the seed for it. Usually it takes a year or two of dormancy before the material pops up again, more insistently choosing me, demanding its growth into a story.

Reading your journal may be helpful when you are stuck for an idea, or just stuck. One treatment for so-called "writer's block" is going back through your journal, picking an entry at random, and assigning it to yourself as a short story or a chapter of a novel. It probably won't turn into any such thing, but the act of trying sometimes helps to dissolve the block. (The hero of *The Horse's Mouth* also said, "When you can't paint—paint.")

For the beginner, keeping a journal is an important way of sharpening the senses, of training yourself to think like a writer. Recording your impressions not only makes you aware of the richness of material in your daily life, it helps train you to look and listen and feel. Well, if you're really a writer, don't you already think like one? Not necessarily. Chances are you have absorbed the same conditioning as other people, and to some degree your work suffers from it.

In order to accept and endure their daily lives, most people learn to blunt their perceptions, to anesthetize their nerve ends, to wear what Samuel Butler called mental and spiritual blinders which cutoff everything but the immediate, expected, assigned behavior. Most people do this even though their style of blinders may vary. One may dress and act stiffly, tightlipped and concentrated on columns of figures. Another may dress and act loose and shaggy, mellow, smiling, and concentrated on nothing. But they are twins, hiding from self-knowledge, from pain, from feeling and thinking beyond the minimum for survival, a minimum which shrinks along with their capacity for full, aware humanity.

The creative person, in the arts, in living, must remove these blinders. This is a long, hard process which is never completed, except by some mystics or, in flashes, by some geniuses. Keeping a journal is a prod, a reminder to look at experience, feel it totally, know it, cherish it, understand it, use it. This is an exciting process, but don't be surprised if, at least in the beginning, it is a very painful one. Write the pain in your journal too. It may contain your best seeds.

After a while, this opening up process becomes a closing in on process. This is a paradox, but I seem to find that most truths have a way of expressing themselves as paradoxes. The creative person, fully opened to possibilities, fully aware, begins to be able to take aim, to cut through distractions and hit—like a dart piercing center target—

just the material she or he can use. This is a different kind of concentration, not narrowly confined by blinders, but truly free.

Sometimes other parts of your life interrupt, stun, stop your writing. These are not "blocks" but disruptions: an exhausting job, small children, illness, divorce, death—crises when the writing routine you have established is suddenly blown to bits. Again. During such times, and they may last weeks, months, or even years, your journal is indispensable, and I can't think of any crisis, short of imprisonment with no writing materials, that would make it impossible to write in your journal for at least half an hour a day. This kind of journal writing keeps your connection with your writer self and may even help you keep your sanity.

(If I acknowledge these disruptions only in passing, it is not to minimize them. On the contrary. Only a tiny minority of the human race has ever been able even to imagine its potential for work beyond what was necessary for bare survival, let alone try to use that potential. You and I belong to that lucky minority. We can only meet obstacles and disruptions the way human beings have always done, a way which can be summed up in very few words: we do what we can.)

Whatever your living and writing conditions, frequent writing in your journal is as helpful as daily running is for an athlete. During especially good writing times, you may not even think of picking up your journal, but it is a good idea, even then, to write a sentence or two describing something you have seen or remembered each day. Smooth times may be especially fertile for the seeds of some future novel, and you don't want to ignore and drop the seed meant to become the novel you will write ten years from now.

I also use my journal as an evaluator, keeping an account of what I'm writing, how it's going, how well I'm managing my life in order to get my work done. I want to understand the process, so I write about writing. I usually do this at night just before I go to sleep, in a quiet few minutes of thinking about how I used the day. Sometimes this evaluation has a way of turning into a list of resolutions for shaping up my work and myself, and I'm sure that someday, if I decide to read my journals, I'll get a few laughs from seeing an identical list of exhortations to myself showing up every couple of months: start writing earlier! lose ten pounds!

Finally the journal is a safe repository for seeds which otherwise you might talk about too freely. I never talk about what I'm writing, and I never talk about ideas for writing. I'm not afraid of ideas being "stolen"; you can't use a seed unless it has stolen you. The danger is that most of my ideas sound stupid when I tell them. What if Dostoevsky had told a friend, "I've got this idea for a novel about a student who kills his landlady. . ." and had gotten, for response, a frown, a yawn, a shrug? Would he have gone ahead anyway and written Crime and Punishment? Maybe, but I don't take chances.

There may be even greater danger if your ideas sound terrific: the danger of talking them out, dissipating the energy you need to shape the material into a story. I've been told by a couple of writers that talking about what they're writing, even showing pages of it in rough draft as it comes out of the typewriter, inspires them, that instant and constant response nourishes them. If this is true for you, ignore what I said about talking only to your journal. But I warn you, it is true for very few writers, and fewer fiction writers. I have reached this conclusion after years of listening to brilliant talk about novels that somehow never got finished.

Implicit in this warning about talking it out is a warning against letting anyone read your journal. In recent years journal keeping has become a popular, shared activity. Classes are given, groups meet and read entries to each other. This may be very pleasant and very helpful to nonwriters, on the level of therapy and communication. It may encourage some interesting writing. But it is dangerous for anyone who aims to write something beyond the journal. I used to read the journals of my students, to prod them and encourage them. Sometimes I encouraged reading journal entries aloud in small groups and discussing their possibilities for stories. Now I think that was a mistake. I believe what Thoreau said about his journals, that there should be something raw and rough about them. Who can pour out what's really raw and rough, knowing that tomorrow night it will be read aloud to a group? Not.

Yet didn't Thoreau, Tolstoy, Virginia Woolf, Henry James, Arnold Bennett, Samuel Butler and many other famous writers expect their journals to be published some day? Yes. Did this knowledge hamper their spontaneity, make them smooth the rough parts? We'll never know. An experienced, highly developed, confident, famous writer may be able to write freely whatever comes to mind, regardless of future readers. But few beginners can be totally honest, free and unselfconscious unless their journals are kept private.

7. Warning: a theme is not a seed.

Theme is the central idea imbedded in a story. It is what holds the best literature together, what Dorothy Sayers in The Mind of the Maker calls "God the Father" of the creative trinity. Good books contain one or more themes which shape and give meaning to the story. The definition of a great novel, a classic, is one which is so thematically rich that it gets better each time we read it; we recognize more as we become capable of understanding more. That fact gives a lot of trouble to literature teachers who construct courses with titles like *Marriage in the Nineteenth Century English Novel*. A good book keeps breaking out of the course outline.

Theme is the backbone of a good novel. But, as in the human embryo, the backbone is not apparent in the early stages after conception.

By all means, think about life and write down all your ideas about life in your journal. But remember, a theme, an idea, is not a seed. If you start with a theme, you may get a lecture or a sermon, but you will seldom get a novel. Or, if you do manage to finish the novel, it is likely to be what Sayers called a "Father ridden" book, written by an author who tries "to impose the idea directly upon the mind and senses, believing that this is the whole of the book. "(Such sermons in fiction are often perpetrated by writers for children and should be listed among the nastier forms of child abuse.)

I once knew a creative writing teacher who told his students to choose a common saying like "Honesty is the best policy," or "He who hesitates is lost," or "Love conquers all," then write a story which illustrated that theme. The results were stories in varying stages of rigor mortis. The teacher complained about the lack of talent in his classes. I think his assignment smothered whatever talent was there.

There are exceptions, of course, like Uncle Tom's Cabin, which Stowe wrote directly from a theme: slavery is evil. It is a powerful novel, no more contrived or sentimental than others of its time, and much better than most. But it came out of an extraordinary moment in history, erupting with the heat of long compressed injustice. As such, it is not a model to apply widely.

I'm not saying that a writer of fiction should not have ideas, convictions, commitment. I can't imagine a writer without conviction writing anything worth reading. I agree with James Baldwin: "All novels are protest novels." In section one I pointed out how Tolstoy, Flaubert, Stendhal and Dreiser got seeds from sensational news items; now I will also remind you that their protagonists, Anna Karenina, Emma Bovary, Julien Sorel and Clyde Griffiths, were in full (if confused and suicidal) rebellion against intolerably unjust, complacent and destructive societies. There's no way a writer can write without exposing his or her convictions. But the themes of a writer will be and should be held in the story as salt is held in suspension in a glass of water the salt no longer distinguishable as salt, but all of the water salty.

The writing of a novel is a voyage of discovery, and you may not begin to know what you are writing about until you are into the third rewrite. Even after the book is finished, published, almost for gotten, some reader may tell you about something, an idea in the book, that you were not conscious of putting there. What went into the novel was chosen in obedience to something deeper than your conscious sense of what you were writing about. That's why you write fiction, for the sake of discovering some deeper truth than facts. And that's why it is important not to fence in your exploration with a too early commitment to a theme.

Having said that, I am confronted by an entry in the notebooks of Henry James, a paragraph which starts, "What is there in the idea of too late ..." and which ends, "... the wasting of life ... There may be the germ of a situation in this, but it obviously requires digging out." Clearly a statement of theme, which several years later became incarnated with variations in such masterpieces as The Ambassadors and "The Beast in the Jungle."

I could call this the exception which proves the rule (but I won't).

I could point out that he couldn't go ahead with this theme until it was later activated by real seeds, incidents, images observed and

21

documented in later notebook entries. Or I could and will just say that this example proves there is no unbreakable rule I can give you for getting a story started. And I still think Henry James would agree with me that, in most cases, it's safer to start with the image, anecdote or incident called the seed, then let it grow into the themes inherent in it and in you.

8. How much planning?

Some writers whose work I respect say they never plan, that planning kills. I don't doubt their sincerity, but I can't believe them. Planning is making decisions. The writer who plunges into a novel with, "I first saw Janice in summer of 1962 ..." has made three planning decisions before writing those words: the choice of first person point of view, the choice of two characters, and the choice of a time. The question is not, should you plan, but how much should you plan? How many decisions can you make before you start?

The answer to this question is, of course, an individual one, varying from writer to writer and from book to book. As a beginner, you should know the full range of planning possibilities, because one of the most crippling myths believed by beginners is that the novelist plunges into writing a book with nothing but an inspired vision and a kind of mad energy.

You may have tried one this way, going pretty far into it on inspiration and black coffee. But chances are that about halfway in, if not sooner, your energy began to wane, certain components of character began to blur, strands of plot became tangled, and you began to hear the ominous creeping in of cold doubt that you really are a novelist after all. At this point you gave up ... again.

Sometimes I have thought that if I could go without sleep or food for about six weeks, in solitary confinement and total silence, writing without stopping, I could go straight from seed to finished novel, and the result would be an extraordinary book which I had lived whole as I wrote it. Sometimes, in my less demanding fantasies, I have wished that a novel were like a painting, so that at least I could step back from it occasionally while working on it, viewing the whole all at once.

But a novel is not a painting, it is not a short story, which you can and should jump into with only minimal decisions. It is not likesome poems, which, though they may suggest much, can be read in a few minutes and held whole in the mind.

A novel is more like as symphony, opera, oratorio. It exists in time, it goes by you like sound dying out as you write on, so that it is very hard to keep in touch with the whole thing as you are writing it. Unlike the inspired energy that flies through the first draft of some poems, the force which drives a novel through the first draft must be more steady. Not like a bird taking off, but more like a mule which can bear the weight of the many elements of the novel over the long haul.

People who say planning kills forget that many of the nineteenth century novels we most admire were planned, blocked out in a very cool, uninspired manner. They had to be, because they were usually serialized in current magazines, appearing chapter by chapter every week or every month. Each chapter was widely, avidly read, and the author could not change her mind in the middle and decide to make her hero a different person entirely nor revive a character she had killed three chapters back. These books do suffer somewhat from the demands of the magazines, for instance the artificial suspense contrived at the end of each chapter, to whet the readers' appetite for the next issue. But no one can say that the planning stopped Dickens and Dostoevsky from writing vivid, deeply moving and true novels.

Most novelists do plan. They may have crashed through their first novels without much planning, but only because they didn't know how. Once they learn better, they try to make as many decisions as possible before starting the rough draft. Those who plan wholly in their heads call it thinking. Those, like me, who think on paper, call it planning.

You can at best make only a few decisions, forming only a bare outline consciously, still leaving most of the decisions for the unconscious to deal with in the process of the writing. A plan just supports the unconscious and may help insure that the unconscious doesn't collapse from doubt, fear and overwork halfway through.

9. Take notes.

I carry 3X5 cards with me everywhere. If I see, hear, or think something interesting, I jot it down on a card which I later paste in my journal. If the card suggests a story, I drop it into a catchall box on my desk, where it lies half-forgotten. Some of the cards in that box are many years old.

Ideas that are likely to turn into novels are magnetic; they attract other ideas, other scribbles about them on more cards. When I begin to accumulate many note cards on one subject, I segregate these cards and give them their own little box. I usually have three or four card boxes labeled with limp working titles like "Girl With Cat." These collections of cards might turn into novels.

Most of them don't. Eventually the cards are dumped back into the catchall box. Some become characters or situations in other novels. Some shrink into short stories. But there's always one box which continues to attract cards, enough cards to attract my attention and make me see that a subject has chosen me.

A subject for a novel usually takes at least two years to form, from the first seed to the time when it begins to crowd other ideas out of my mind. (This process can go on while I'm working on something else.) I suspect that a novel requires a long period of unconscious development after the first glimmer is noted, a fusing with related elements, a gathering of weight. It is as if the novel is writing itself underground and I must wait for it to be done before I begin the conscious process of digging it up.

When this first planning decision has been made, this choice of the seed, I settle down in earnest to scribbling on cards. During my regular working hours, three to four morning hours six days a week, I sit and let things come: images, people, bits of dialogue, incidents, names, places. After the concentrated effort of working hours, the ideas keep coming while I'm doing other things, not trying at all, and I keep jotting down whatever pops into my mind.

Here are some examples, chosen at random from the stacks of planning cards for the novel I am working on now.

Table and chairs near the window, a rudimentary note about the setting, a special problem in this novel because the point-of-view character is blind.

Each memory must be interesting in itself. Can I do that? This is a worry card. I write lots of these.

What would she have done if she hadn't been blinded? She had a typing job in S.F. and a boyfriend she was going to marry. When she heard the boyfriend was dead she felt a great sense of relief and realized she didn't really want to marry him. Or does the boyfriend leave her after she is blinded?

This is about the longest card I ever write, and this particular one turned out to be useless. I changed my mind and discarded everything on it before I started writing.

Facing being totally alone, alone. Then instantly leaping beyond that to know I am never alone. I have never done anything by myself before, not anything that counts. I am starting to identify with the protagonist here, putting myself into her skin, a move which eventually became the use of first person point of view, a decision I had been strongly resisting.

At home, everything new, like a department store, no human smell. Nomads in a department store like a movie (story?) of that man who lived at Macy's, another setting card, trying to suggest an image by referring to an odorless department store-window home. Setting cards would normally be more visual.

Father like————————————,————————————,
_____? Kind to her, but something brutal in him. He helps her but also leaves things around which she trips over. Squandering her money in wild schemes. No imagination. Always doing for you what you don't need.

His needs? Envies his daughter. Lost youth and freedom.

Restless. This card is a start on a character. (The blanks are people I know.) Obviously a confused card, lumping together character traits that won't fit but which do suggest others.

Lon and Tom meet on campus. A plot card I always knew would be an opening scene in the book.

"I am a survivor," says Tom, "though I never really wanted to survive." He has seen so many people die.

When I got into first draft writing, Tom refused to say this, but I think it was implicit in his other words and acts.

These cards, maybe hundreds of them, are like odd shaped pieces of a jigsaw puzzle, which make no sense in themselves but are part of a total picture. The difference between these notes and a jigsaw puzzle is that my notes don't come in a package with a picture on it, the picture which all the bits will eventually make when they are fitted together. Most of my puzzle pieces will eventually be discarded, and using the ones that are left, I still have only a vague idea of the picture they will make. (If I knew for sure, I probably wouldn't bother to write the book.)

I keep piling up scribbled cards, not worrying if I repeat myself, just letting it all come. Each day I read through the cards and think about them, letting them stimulate more scribbles. It's a pleasant process, full of possibility without drudgery, and I'm sometimes tempted to go on this way forever.

But after a few weeks it begins to take longer to read through the cards than to write new ones, and the new ones only repeat the old ones. Then I know that this part of the planning, this collecting of preliminary scraps, has come to an end. There won't be any fresh ideas to collect until I push myself on to a further stage of planning, closer to the dreaded writing itself.

Next I start sorting through the cards, putting them into related piles. Most cards end up in one of three piles: characters, setting, plot. There are a few leftover cards with general notes regarding how I see the form and slant and tone of the book, vague glimpses of themes. I keep them too, but in a pile at a safe distance, where they can't start pushing characters around or twisting the plot out of its natural shape. I'm not ready for them yet.

Making these three stacks is an easy, logical, but giant step in organization, and reading through each stack, I can see much more of the shape the book might take. And I generally can see a way of adding at least another week's worth of scribbles to each stack before I'm ready to go on to the next phase of dealing with each stack separately.

Don't take that last paragraph too literally. Of course, none of these three elements is really separate from the other two, so I can't really work on only one stack at a time. It is only for the sake of discussion that I want to treat them separately, as if I could.

10. Setting: Place and Time

If you worry about over planning, I promise you that you can't overplay setting. You can write out pages and pages of details describing the place and time of your story, and the effort will add to your sense of security without detracting one bit from your urge to write or your spontaneity of invention.

Setting is probably the easiest to plan and the hardest to write. Ifs hard to write because many readers, spoiled by movies and TV, used to getting the whole scene in a flash, won't read long passages of description. So you have to select details of scene with great skill (unless you are a conscious rebel against this generalization and plan to bring back lavish, long descriptions). But setting is easy to plan because it's mainly the filling in of background, probably with familiar objects and locations you can use with little change.

This doesn't mean you can be careless in the planning. Ford Maddox Ford once said that he had to know the shape of all the doorknobs or he wouldn't be able to get his characters in and out of rooms. He exaggerated, but not much. It's probably a good idea to write out the descriptions you know you won't put into the book or at least to draw diagrams. It all depends on the settings and on how you are using them.

If one brief scene in your novel is set in a restaurant you know very well, a hangout of yours, you may think you don't have to plan at all because your familiarity with the place will come through in the writing. Maybe. But there's always the risk that, knowing it so well, you'll assume too much, tell the reader too little, and end up with the reader feeling cheated or lost. So it wouldn't hurt to at least draw a floor plan, during which exercise you may discover that you've never really looked at the place.

Ella Price's journal was set on a composite of various campuses where I had taught, but mostly on the one I saw daily while I was writing. Since certain elements of all schools are pretty much the same, I could cheat a little, merely mentioning "the classroom," "the halls," "the parking lot," and letting the reader fill in images and get on with the story. I drew a diagram of the cafeteria seating pattern, which came from a college I hadn't seen for some time. The peace march in which Ella participated was an actual one, the Vietnam Day March of 1965. I described it as accurately as I could, even to the different colored uniforms of the Berkeley (tan) and Oakland (blue) police. I treated it as an historic event. Everything that Ella saw actually happened that night. I had written it all down in my journal. I didn't go back to the journal and copy my report but visualized my memories at the typewriter. I think it came out fresher that way. In that case, my planning for the peace march setting had been done three years before.

If the whole novel is set on a certain block of your old horns town, you probably should diagram it carefully, describing the house of each character, the shops, the street, the traffic pattern Otherwise you may have trouble moving your characters around 0I even knowing what they can do and how long it takes them to do it Place dictates much more of action than beginning writers realize. For example, if two characters are arguing while in a canoe, one of them can't make a dramatic yet dignified exit.

It is in the smaller details of place that you will mix the real with the invented. A house, for instance, may start as one you have actually seen, but then you can change it to suit the action: shift doorways, increase or decrease the number and size of rooms, change location of windows. Your hero must be able to see the south corner of the garden from his bedroom window, for instance, if you're going to have him glance out at the right moment to see his wife passionately kissing his father... or his sister... or whatever complex dilemma you are about to inflict upon him.

Chekhov once said that if you describe a gun hanging on the wall in the first scene, by the third scene it had better go off. In other words, the setting is inseparable from the action, ideally, it should seem as if only certain types of characters could perform these particular acts in this particular setting.

The novel How Green Was My Valley comes close to this ideal. When I think of that book, I see the great slag heap which year by year grows, encroaching upon the houses of the miners, until industrial exploitation wipes out a whole way of life. Obviously those people, that story, could not exist anywhere else. The slag heap makes a great symbol, doesn't it? But it wasn't invented to be a symbol. It's a real slag heap, sharply and deeply observed by the author as part of the setting, and he probably didn't see that he had such a powerful symbol until he was well into the writing.

Novels set in a less special place should have the same inevitability and clarity, and one way to get it is careful planning, down to the smallest detail.

Sometimes beginners think their problems will be solved if they set their novel in a more "interesting" place, a big city instead of the suburb of a small one. This can seem like an easy way out. But in writing, the easy way out usually turns out to be like a window on the tenth story, from which the whole book falls, splat.

Experienced writers are not immune. Recently I read a novel set in New York City, which took the central character on a shopping trip through Brentano's, through Bergdorf's, up along the edge of Central Park, and so on. As I read I wondered what editor let the author get away with this, assuming that "everyone" knows Manhattan. For this was not a setting; it was a list. The fact that the book was probably aimed at an audience of women in the same rut as the heroine was no excuse.

Even when the writer does all the planning to make the city vivid and sure, there's the danger of a famous setting taking over. An example is another recent novel, set in London and written by an author who spent four loving years there, awed by a place whose history and monuments could just gobble up a novel. That's what happened in this case. Characters were moved from Trafalgar Square to The Tower to Westminster and so on, not a list, each place impeccably and vividly evoked. But reading the book was like taking a ride on one of those tourist buses, seeing places where the author stood his characters like fashion models posed under Bugbane, when they could just as well have been posed on the Golden Gate Bridge or the lower slopes of Annapurna. Nothing that happened had to happen where it did. The characters and their story paled in the strong light the author cast on his setting.

Skillful writers often suggest urban complexity by confining their story to a part of the city. Doris Lessing evoked 1960's London in The

Four-Gated City with characters who hardly ever left the baghouse where the heroine lived with assorted members of a family and their friends. It seems that the more narrow the boundaries of your place, the deeper you can go.

This might mean that if your novel is set in some little town you know well but no one else ever heard of, you're lucky. If your boundaries are very narrow, your place very removed from excitement, your town life very "ordinary," you just have less surface material to handle. Remember, Madame Bovary couldn't have been set in amore ordinary place. Minute observation and description brought out the extraordinary quality of its ordinariness.

Maybe you write fantasy, in which case you think you can avoid all these problems by putting in the doorknobs anywhere you like. The problem here is that this freedom is gained at the price of a huge weight of responsibility. For, if you set the story in a place outside any world we know, you may be free from the carping reader who says, "I knew the Berkeley campus in 1965, and there was no Zeilerbach Hall yet," but you are responsible for creating a whole new world which must be consistent in every detail. This means a prolonged planning stage. It demands hard thinking, certainty about your intent, familiarity with every carefully thought out detail of setting. Otherwise you will end up like one of my writing students, who created a world without gravity, then built to a climactic scene in which the villain falls to his death.

When I created an island for *The Kin of Ata Are Waiting For You,* I covered my walls with maps, charts, drawings. I had to know details of life that I never have to bother with in a "realistic" novel: where is the water supply? how is clothing made? what sanitary practices? how severe are the winters? how is food grown? cooked? eaten? On and on, hundreds of details that had to be consistent with the themes I was exploring, had to add up to, as Conrad says, a place I could believe in. For if I couldn't, who else would? From this ocean of precise, consistent detail I extracted drops of description to put here and there in the action, without long passages of description and explanation that would destroy the momentum I had to keep if I were to give the reader the emotional experience essential to the book's credibility. I had freedom from searching for the right word to show a building which might be familiar to my readers, but I bought that freedom with hours of painstaking construction.

If you write an historical novel, you have some help in creating another world, from writers who came before you. You will have to study many books during your planning stage. You will have to come to know the place and time, down to the smallest details of daily life which are knowable. But if you are thorough in your research, you will know about as much as anyone else can know. After all, there are no eyewitnesses, only scholars who will be dependent on the same sources you use, and who may even be willing to help you find material.

In a sense, we are all always writing historical novels since every story takes place in a certain historical time. Like place, time should be so thoroughly meshed with events that the action seems inevitable for that time and yet contains something of the timeless in human affairs. If your novel is set in the present, you will have to see that "present" with a clear eye, knowing it in a conscious way, knowing its special quality. Probably a fish never knows that it lives its whole life in water, because it never really thinks about it, can't get out of it. Well, you must really think about it and, in a way, stand out of it while you're in it.

But if you get all the details right—language, clothes, customs—isn't your novel likely to be dated awfully fast? Maybe. And yet, certain types of people with certain attitudes doing certain things are part of a certain time.

In 1972 the publisher who finally accepted my four year old Ella Price's journal wanted me to cut out the peace march. "Too dated. Too much of the sixties flavor." I felt the scene was crucial, actually the climax of the book, where Ella learns that ideas and thoughts lead to action, and where I finally got her out of her own head, out of her own narrow world. "Yes, yes," said my publisher, "but can't you substitute some other event or action?" I thought about that, asked for suggestions. But my final answer was, no, the peace march belongs there, dated or not. And now that interest in the sixties is reviving, some people read it for the flavor of that peace march.

But even if they didn't, who says a book has to last forever? Sinclair Lewis used to say that whenever he was told about a new

31

book, he waited two years. If it was still around, then he read it. Good advice. But if it isn't still around twenty or thirty years later, that doesn't mean it was a bad book. It was good for a certain moment in time. It lived and it died. That is true of all life, and all books. Understanding Shakespeare demands hard, careful reading with the help of footnotes, and his plays have been around only about three hundred years ... a moment in time!

I've often heard psychologists say that writers write as a protest against their own mortality, seeking to defeat their personal death by leaving behind something eternal. I don't, and I think any writer who does is hampered by a debilitating delusion. You can't leave behind any material object that will last for long. Even words don't last, but become meaningless as language changes. What is left, what is eternal, is the effect of your work, of your life, put out, done, and diffused through all of life. Its value will depend on the honesty and depth and truth you reached through doing it. That is what lasts, not any little object or cluster of words with your name on it.

So. After that little sermon, I'll go back to mundane writing problems and contradict myself by telling you that sometimes it is better to cut out the topical.

My novel Prisoners (unpublished as of this writing) was set in 1972, and since my characters were politically active, I involved them in the presidential campaign and other political issues of that year. By the time I finished the book, all my carefully collected details of a presidential campaign which had seemed an historic mountain (or pit) had become a bit dim. Yet I thought that, like Ella's peace march, these details were an integral part of the story and must be left in, with the hope that last year's stale news would become interesting historical detail in ten more years. But a friend who read the manuscript finally made me see that this case was different. I found that I could easily take out the election and other topical parts, substituting more general, perennial political issues that did just as well without distracting a reader who was ignorant of specific issues of that year. Does that mean I wasted all that time getting the election details right? Certainly not. The emotional weight of those details was still there.

Writers find ways to get rid of the topical while keeping the authentic. Catcher in the Rye seems to be written in an authentic teenage voice. Yet, if you examine it, word by word, you will find that Salinger uses none of the topical teenage slang of the time when he wrote it. If he had, it would have felt dated and stale by the time it was published, for nothing ages into triteness so fast as this month's high school slang, and its actual vocabulary is too narrow for more than a few pages of story, let alone a whole novel. What Salinger did was to create a language, a tone and rhythm suggesting that slang, taken from it and from some emotional base of adolescence. How he did it I don't know, part of planning, part of rewriting. If he was lucky, he hit on it as an early planning decision.

Some writers remove from their fiction any specific reference to styles, like hemlines of dresses, that might quickly become dated. That's all right if these details would be distracting and can be cutout without thinning out the background too much. But be careful not to lose essential details.

Just remember, you must know everything well before you can know what to discard. You must cover pages with material you will not finally put into the book. That doesn't mean you don't use it. Itis still there, must be there, an invisible foundation which gives authority to the story. The planning done on setting is never wasted.

Nothing is ever wasted. If it has been thought through and written, it is still there, in every word which does not mention it.

11. Characters

Your stack of character cards probably looks like a pile of faded, overexposed snapshots of friends, relatives and acquaintances, many of them in unflattering poses. That seems to be what most of us start with in creating characters. Except for *Kin of Ata,* where all the characters were allegorical types, I always start with someone I know or once knew, or someone I have at least seen.

When possible I change the appearance, occupation, even the sex of the original character model because I don't want to cause anyone pain or embarrassment. But these changes aren't always possible. Sometimes the fact that the central character model is a female, Jewish dentist determines so much of what happens to her and what her response is that any variation in this bundle of characteristics would destroy the credibility of my story. This is a hard question. If necessary I let her stand as she is and try to disguise events or setting so that even if the model recognizes herself in the character, it is unlikely that anyone else will, and I will have saved her some embarrassment. So far the models I've used have not recognized themselves, or if they have, they've kept quiet about it.

What does happen frequently is that people mistakenly name themselves or someone they know as the model for a character which has nothing to do with them. My Ella Price has an affair wither English teacher, superficially a composite of several men I knew, but in a deeper sense made up of parts of myself. I was still teaching at the time it was published, and I was repeatedly stopped in the halls by giggling gossip lovers who winked and said they recognized so-and-so as the teacher, each of them naming a different man and only laughing harder when I honestly told them that the models for the character were not on that campus. More recently friend of mine read a manuscript and astonished me with a hurt accusation that I had modeled a certain character on her. Aside from being the same age and graduates of the same university, my friend and my character had nothing whatever in common, and I can't imagine what made my friend attribute the Song list of my character's failures to herself.

When I choose a model, I'm actually choosing, not that person, but a particular quality. It might be a certain vulnerability or passion that I sense in her or a strain of daring or of fear that seems likely to lead to certain events, or a particular act she committed which evokes a complex of possibilities.

Once I have that element of character as seen in a real person, I am ready to begin to construct the whole character. I put a sheet of paper in the typewriter and start inventing a dossier: life history, family, education, work, likes and dislikes, mannerisms, speech patterns, physical traits. (Chekhov, who was a doctor, said physical ailments were important components of character... hay fever? athletes foot?) Hardly any of this information will go into the book, but I have to know it before I can make this character speak, move, think, react.

If I know it well, everything the character says or does will expose the traits I've listed.

While you are compiling this imaginary dossier, you will find that the character begins to deviate from the model you started with. Certain traits become exaggerated and others are dropped. You begin to borrow traits from other people you know or to graft on compatible mannerisms or clothes which you invent. Soon the character becomes a composite of traits from the original model, from other people, from your imagination, and from yourself. I always feel that just about every character I invent contains something of me, not always a very admirable part.

The great advantage of detailed character planning is that you can make sure the traits you are combining really fit together, before you start the writing. It's much easier to match up traits while planning than to try to glue together an inconsistent character whose ill-fitting pieces keep coming apart while you are writing. I'm talking about consistency on the simplest level. In other words, while I am adding items to the list in a dossier, I am crossing out earlier listed ones that don't fit, so that I don't end up with a nearsighted person who becomes a marksmanship champion.

It is consistency on a deeper level that writers really worry about. Somerset Maugham once wrote that Julien Sorel in *The Red and the Black* acted out of character when he shot his mistress, doing something that, given his character, he would never have done. I disagree, but his objection brings up the importance of, as E. M. Forsterput it, characters "surprising us in a convincing way." You can't be certain about achieving this deeper consistency during the planning stage or even during the first draft writing; you can try to prepare yourself to reach it, or at least not handicap yourself with incomplete dossiers.

Later, while rewriting, you'll get reader reaction. At that point if more than one person tells you that a character's behavior is incredible, you might have a problem, not only in the structure of the character you've created but in your preparation for his surprisingact. It seems to me that most human beings are, given the right setof circumstances, capable of almost any act. If the act is not convincing, it is likely that you didn't do enough preparatory ground work, either in character revelation or in clarifying the surroundingcircumstances. Or it could be that your conception of the characterchanged during the writing, but you're still trying to force him to do something you had in the original plan. In that case, of course, you must deviate from your plan.

By the way, if a character does something incredible to several trustworthy readers, you can't dismiss their complaints with, "But that's the way it really happened." Nothing happens without cause, either in books or in life. In life the cause is often so obscure to our self-centered, short-range consciousness that we have learned to shrug at what we don't understand and label it accident or coincidence. But in fiction your reader looks for a more apparent consistency and causation. In fiction you arrange facts and fantasy to arrive at truth. What "really" happened is usable only when it fits the pattern of truth you are weaving.

The most often quoted statement on character comes from Aspects of the Novel, where E. M. Forster discusses "round" and "flat" characters, round ones being complex while flat characters are types who can be summed up in one sentence. Dostoevsky's characters, he tells us, are mostly round, while Dickens' characters are mostly flat. Good comic characters are flat, but "a serious or tragic flat character is apt to be a bore." Flat characters are easily recognized and easily remembered but "not as big achievements around ones." Forster concludes, "A novel that is at all complex often requires flat people as well as round ..."

Most novels do turn out to have a mixture of round and flat. But this should not be an issue during the planning phase. Creating character who is a believable person is such a hard thing to do. The more I watch people, the more they amaze me. Totally "flat" and predictable as most of them are, they nevertheless are, simultaneously, deeply "rounder" than the most complex character books. (I used to believe just the opposite, but I think I listen look better now.) I never think of whether I'm going to use a character as a round or a flat. I compile each dossier as if it were for a central character. As the story unfolds, during the writing, son the characters flatten out to fit its shape. And if some of them come more prominent than I expected, I'm ready for them w complete dossier.

What about names for your characters? That seems such a small point, but it is over those little things that we sometimes stumble so I give my characters names as soon as possible. Naming them I free them from the models, gives the characters solidity and identity at the very beginning of formation. But how to choose names?

Should the name express some dominant trait? Henry James thought so and gave a lot of attention to naming characters, mixed effects. I'm not fond of a name like Mrs. Grosse for the fat, simple housekeeper in "Turn of the Screw." Names like hers flatten characters, and unless you're writing an allegory like Pilgrim's Progress you don't want to label and limit your characters. Unless name is very subtle and broadly suggestive, a symbolic name is a lazy way to set the reader for or against a character, like calling your villain something like Maladict Dump. Unless, of course, write comic novels; then you can do a lot with names.

In one book I gave all my characters the names of friends didn't resemble them in any way and were amused to find names in my book. For Ella Price's journal I went through my address book, selecting first names to pair up with last names. Afterward I discovered that Ella's last name carried some symbolic weight in her story. Since making that discovery, I tend to write down the first name that comes into my head. If for some reason my first choice is no good, I write down the next name comes into my head and so on until I find one to which I see objection. Most of the time this random process provides name quite satisfied with, probably because the quick, spontaneous choice comes from a deeper part of me that knows more than I consciously know about my characters and their story. In one I carefully avoided giving a central character any name at all. Narrator and protagonist of *Kin of Ata* remains nameless, to emphasize the universality of his spiritual journey.

I guess you can name your characters anything you want to, so long as their names are consistent with ethnic origins. Just be sure to name them early enough so that while planning you don't have to keep referring to one of them as male-sixty-who-teaches-heroine-swimming-and-looks-like-my-uncle-Matthew.

Finally, what about yourself as character? Many autobiographical novels are built entirely around the author thinly disguised as central character. A few of these novels are great classics. Many others are very good. But thousands (I include ail the unpublished and unfinished ones) are embarrassing, with their romanticized, polished up heroes, paragons of sensitivity and talent, fighting to survive and grow among the clods who seem to make up the rest of the human race.

We're all a little bit self-indulgent, and I have found that placing myself directly in a book brings out a defensive urge to retouch the portrait: I start lying. I can be more honest and more free if I slip into characters based on other models, adding a fragment of my experience here and there in their stories.

What many writers learn is that once they move away from the directly autobiographical, they gain enormous freedom to move, to invent, to see more clearly their subjects and themes, and to work them out without paralyzing self-consciousness.

But why am I warning you? What am I warning you against? If the autobiographical one has chosen you, that's the one you'll have to do. If so, I wish you the passion of D. H. Lawrence or the humor of Samuel Butler to help bring it off. Even if it doesn't come off, you'll have learned whatever it is you have to know before you can go on to the next one.

12. Plot

Keeping plot elements on cards allows you to spread them out, shuffle them, rearrange them, add or subtract incidents to get a general idea of the series of events which will make up your story. You keep doing this, between working on your other two stacks of cards, until you have a series of events or happenings running through the whole story. There will be holes in the series, dubious happenings, or even some places where you haven't the faintest idea what will happen. I wouldn't worry about that. If you've drawn your characters carefully, they may solve some of these problems for you while you're writing the rough draft.

Once you have a fairly complete deck of plot cards, you'll find them grouping themselves into sections. These sections may be short chapters or long segments or both: short parts within long parts. The length of sections and the order they follow will be dictated by the content, by the story itself, and you should get a fair idea of the division of material by the way the cards seem to want to group themselves.

Now you have a series of little stacks of plot cards, like hands dealt in a poker game. You may want to make an outline from them. If you do, be careful not to write too much. A chapter outline should probably resemble the chapter headings in an early novel like Candide: "Chapter I. How Candide was brought up in a fine castle and how he was driven from it," with no more than a few scribbles of the most necessary notes below it. Writing too many .details is moving too close to the rough draft phase. In plot planning, be wary of killing the writing with the planning. I prefer to stick to the cards rather than making an outline on paper. It's easier to make changes or to shift events around, and clipping groups of cards together is enough to remind me of the division into sections. , I did little conscious plot planning for Ella Price's journal, partly because even after writing for eight years, I didn't know how. I knew the beginning and the ending. I knew that Ella would start by entering college and end by leaving her marriage, because that was the situation, the seed, I had observed, and my novel was to be an exploration of how she moved from that beginning to that end. I had decided on no more than four or five definite events between start and finish. I counted on the journal form to save me: if things didn't fit together, I could always add entries or subtract them. Needless to say, that's not why I chose the journal form. The content chose that form. (See section 14.)

Yet, in a sense I had been plot-planning that novel for at least ten years in that I had been assigning journals for my students, and I had been observing in these journals a consistent succession, regardless of age or sex, of emotional stages of learning: fear, anger, confusion, pain, and so on. The first page of that novel was a modified version of an instruction list for journal keeping different from the fiction writer's list in section 6) which I had been handing out for years, and I used it as a guide to get me through the first part of the book.

Later in the book I got into all sorts of trouble that I could have avoided if I had known more about planning. I planned as well as I knew how, then jumped in and struggled, putting myself into Ella's narrow but expanding consciousness and muddling on through.

The Kin of Ata I planned extensively, minutely, for setting, but plot planning was minimal. The book divides into six sections, and I don't believe I wrote down more than a few sentences for each section, describing the main action. Then I visualized while writing, a common habit of writers which you may already have adopted without having to think about \t} You close your eyes and concentrate on the action, walking your characters through it and writing down all the details as they occur. In this way, for instance, I "danced" the dance of the numbers, which on my plot outline was no more than a subheading, "dance of numbers."

I did somewhat more detailed plot cards on Miss Ciardino. The main problem of this book was how to give a recognizable portrait, a long life history of an "ordinary" life without wearying the reader with a long book. The form seemed obvious: an eventful week in her life, with flashbacks, present and past illuminating each other, creating an outline portrait which the reader could fill in. Selecting and matching present action with flashbacks called for more detailed plot planning with notes to myself on how the various elements were to support each other.

The most extensive plot outline I ever made is for the novel I'm working on now. Because this story takes place in only twelve hours and is broken up into gradually shortening sections of stream-of-consciousness flashback, I have had to keep total control over all plot elements, to match up present action with memory, and to show the heroine's change of perception of past and present as the action moves toward climax. I've never done so many detailed plot cards before— and all this for the shortest novel I've written. I suspect that after this one I'll go back to few, brief plot cards for future novels.

You might be the sort of writer who loves his or her story and throughout plot planning remains convinced that it's the most interesting, suspenseful and original story ever written. This conviction is more likely to stick with you if you are writing out of some extraordinary firsthand experience, like a war or a plane crash or a kidnapping, or if you are inventing a fantasy world or a mystery. But if you are writing one of the quieter, hidden dramas of so-called ordinary life, this may be one of the points at which you begin to feel great uncertainty, a horrible sinking feeling that your story is not important or interesting to anyone but you, and right now you're not sure about you.

Chances are you are suffering merely a failure of nerve that may come several times, at any stage of the writing. There is a difference between a cool appraisal which tells you something won't do, and this sudden attack of mild to medium panic. I have never gotten through a book without several attacks of this panic, like malarial tremors that shake me up but then pass. The first tremor usually comes during plot planning.

I guess all writers must learn to live with the doubts that occasionally flare up into a fever of panic. Try to ignore panic and doubt until it passes. Tell yourself that this plot, whatever it is, has for the moment chosen you. You don't have to stick to it if you find out later, in the rough draft writing, that you can do something better. But right now it's what you see as a framework of events, a line to hang onto. So accept it; don't ask yourself any muddling questions. Just get on with it.

13. Research

If you're writing an historical novel or a science fiction novel with a plot based on certain technological possibilities, you've probably done library research ahead of time, and the book has actually sprung from the research. But almost every other kind of novel also demands research of a sort, which is indicated by questions that arise during the planning stage. It is a good idea to get some answers to these questions before you begin your rough draft because often your research will show you that important elements of your novel must be changed. So while you're planning, you should keep a stack of cards on which you write questions on technical points.

Your research may be as simple as revisiting a setting you are using, just to make sure you get it right. Or it may mean a trip to the library to check out the exact date on which a real, historical event happened. While planning Miss Ciardino I revisited the Mission District of San Francisco, where I grew up, and I made a point of checking records to make sure the Mission Branch of the public library actually had been completed at the time my heroine was supposed to have lived near it.

Research may mean interviewing someone who works in the same occupation as one of your characters, visiting the person on the job, if possible. Or you may need to watch a procedure, like renting a concert hall or setting up a blood transfusion. This kind of research is fun because it's one of the few parts of writing that isn't lonely; you get to see people, often people you wouldn't otherwise meet. You'll probably enjoy going to various places, telling people what you're doing, asking for a little knowledge to give authenticity to your story. I look back fondly on the afternoon I spent at the local police station, "getting arrested" by an officer who "used to do a little writing myself." (Of course, there was a part of me that had to keep working on what a real arrest would feel like, but if, as one writer has said, every honest writer should expect someday to spend some time in prison, I can look forward to experiencing the totality.)

Sometimes you'll run into resistance, even what seems like paranoia, when you try to go through regular channels to get information. You can explain over and over that you write fiction, that your story is already formed in your mind, and that all you want to see is the form filled out by a certain official so that you can give authenticity to a particular scene. No matter what you say, the strangers you contact may remain convinced that you are writing an expose of their business or government agency. Several times people have inadvertently given me material and ideas in their very resistance tome.

When you encounter this resistance, you'll just have to make ales direct approach. Usually you can ask around until you find friend who has a contact who knows someone else who knows venereal disease tracker or a steeple jack or whomever you need for your research. When you approach people through these unofficial channels, they usually turn out to be willing to talk and talk, since most people like to talk shop and may never have been asked to before. They may even develop an investment in your book, a feeling that they are participating in its creation. You'll have fun, and you may even make new friends.

You'll probably pick up more information than you need for your novel, but even what is not "used" gives a firm underpinning to your story. And I'd be surprised if you don't pick up extra material for your journal which will someday ripen into a short story or add character to a novel.

There's a temptation to talk too much about your novel with these research people, since they will be very interested in at least certain technical parts of the book. Tell them a few plot element but no more than you have to. Otherwise, you might talk it all out. If you explain why you are reserved, they usually understand. R< member, you're there to hear them talk, not to be so flattered by their interest in the writing process that you spill all your ideas an dissipate the mysterious energy that makes you want to write them down.

You should go to a research person with a list of specific questions, but don't stick too closely to the list. If the person begins to ramble off from your questions, let him. You can always take u your specific questions again later. Try to arrange an informal meeting, taking a couple of people out to eat or drink, where the will talk to each other, raising questions you never thought of. One of the best research sessions I ever had came on a Friday night spent with several tired juvenile probation officers. They drank, exchanged stories, unwound from the week's load of work and frustration, and soon were going back twenty years in their stories, arguing joking, forgetting I was there, yet playing to me too. If I had stuck to the list of questions I came with, I would never have got what really needed.

14. Form

I hope you've heard the old saying that form and content cannot be separated, that form grows out of content. Ideally, by the time you have gone this far into planning, the decision about form has made itself, chosen itself as inevitably as your story chose you However, I'll add these few direct suggestions because sometime the beginning writer doesn't know what options exist.

Some beginners assume that a novel should be a straightforward chronological narrative, split into chapters, beginning at the beginning and moving on to the end. This is the form of the class nineteenth century novel, and it is probably the hardest to do, just as the sonnet is one of the hardest forms of poetry to write because the form has been exploited and perfected by masters. I don't mean you shouldn't attempt the straight narrative form, if it's right for you, no matter how often it's been done. I used it for King of Ata because the content demanded it: fantasy often is best held in the firm, familiar shape of a traditional form. Just be aware that there are other forms, and don't worry if your novel won't fit the older form you think of when you think of "The Novel."

One of the earliest novels was written as a series of letters. I borrowed that form for Prisoners: a series of letters between two people who had never met, followed by a series of scenes after they meet, alternating point of view in a form which paralleled the letters and cast new light on them.

Other novels have been done as journals kept by one of the characters, like my Ella Price's journal. The journal form was an inevitable choice that came with the seed, growing out of my teaching years. I did another novel almost wholly as a series of interviews, borrowing detective story techniques to illuminate a mystery of character and situation, a problem to which there is no "solution, "no simple culprit to be brought to justice.

My first attempt at a novel was a series of stories, each complete in itself but connected by a theme that bound them all together and led to a climax involving all of them. I was probably influenced by Sherwood Anderson's *Winesburg, Ohio* and William March's *Company K*. It's an interesting form, which March explained was like putting a lot of separate portraits on a wheel, then spinning the wheel until all the separate bits blur into a moving design. I'm afraid my wheel jerked and bumped, and my admittedly blurred story wasn't a design achieved by movement but the product of my getting dizzy from the effort. But I learned a lot, and now I see that unpublishable book as my first move from short story writing to novel writing.

A novel can start anywhere, at the end if you like, then jump back and forth among flashbacks to fill in the story. It can take place in eleven different countries or inside someone's head. It can cover eight generations or eight hours.

These days novels often imitate other forms, like autobiography or history. They borrow from the mass media, imitating interviews or even cartoons. Sometimes they read like technical reports or notes on a scientific experiment. Some are almost all dialogue like movie script, while others are streams of poetic, run together thoughts, with hardly a word spoken. And some novels mix together all these devices, then splash them onto the page with eccentric typographical tricks.

But maybe I didn't have to tell you all that. Maybe you're a well-read beginner, sophisticated about modern form. If so, you must watch out for another danger. Don't be tempted to choose a form (instead of letting it be chosen by your content) just because it is unusual or interesting or because some other writer was called a genius for doing something so odd, different, avant-garde. You may end up with a sterile imitation of your genius model. Or you may write something in a form which is a passing fad and quickly becomes quaint or tiresome.

When I studied music, I made all the mistakes anyone could. In composition class, I wanted to write truly "modern" music, so I concocted dissonant and complex pieces which the college orchestra found unplayable. Even I, to my great embarrassment, was unable to play one of my compositions at the piano (my instrument) without stumbling over its disjointed obscurities. The only piece I wrote that was any good was the one for an assignment to do a pop tune, a ballad. I did a good piece because that was the kind of music I knew. It was there I should have started because that was where I was at eighteen, having come from a background almost devoid of classical music. But I wanted to be up there with Stravinsky (now that I knew he was superior to Cole Porter!) speaking his language, which was not my language. Whatever my language was to be, I would have to grow up to it starting from where I was. But I was too insecure, too self-rejecting. My intentions were good; my methods were self-defeating.

For some writers, imitation of admired models is a necessary phase in their development, along with imitation of eccentric forms. But sooner or later you must abandon the warmed-over versions of what another writer would do, and get back to yourself. Poor as they seem, your story and your form are all you have to start with.

If your story wants to form itself as a series of traffic tickets interspersed with doctors' prescriptions and trial transcripts, let it. But if it starts unreeling like a novel by Jane Austen, accept that form and don't worry about being old-fashioned. Maybe Jane Austen is due for a comeback as the next avant-garde movement.

15. Point of View

I was tempted to skip this subject entirely, hoping that the innocent beginner might make free, uninformed but instinctively right decisions on point of view if he or she were not confused and corrupted by knowing that such a term existed. But I was persuaded by former students of mine that avoiding the subject would only be tossing the unsuspecting beginner into the jaws of those sharks lying out there in the ocean of creative writing classes, waiting to snap, "You shifted point of view!" then chewing up your work before you can figure out what the term means.

Point of view doesn't mean how you feel about the world or what your political connections are or what your opinion on a particular issue is. As used by writers it means, who tells the story? Simple to state, but more complicated to explain and apply, because implicit in this question are others. How clearly present is the author? How directly do we sense her voice? What attitude does she adopt toward her characters? What tonal effects come out of answers to these questions?

Who tells the story? Well, you do, don't you? Yes and no. Let's think about storytellers, old-fashioned storytellers, the kind you become when you are telling a story to a child, a fairy tale or a story you make up as you go along. "Once upon a time ..." you begin, describing the characters, telling what they did, what each of them thought or didn't think, what each knew and didn't know. You know everything and everyone, how the story starts and ends, and what it all means. You may not tell everything—some things you hold back for suspense—but you, like God, know all and see all. You are, in writer's jargon, the omniscient point of view. That means you use shifting third person (he, she, they, it) point of view: "Jack hid in the oven, quivering with fear. The giant knew something human was near, but he couldn't figure out where Jack was. And his wife wouldn't tell because she liked little boys like Jack, and she didn't want her husband to eat him up." Then you stepped in as author to comment on the action: "Wouldn't it be terrible if the giant found Jack!" Many fairy tales and many nineteenth century novels are written from this omniscient point of view, but by no means all.

There were always storytellers who told stories as if they person ally had seen them happening. "As I was walking down the road, I saw ..." They had learned that what we call first person point of view had certain advantages, mainly giving the story authenticity. Somerset Maugham used this type of first person narration, putting himself, as author and man, on the edge of the action as observer, telling the story as he "watched" it happening. Turgenev did it in his "Hunting Sketches." Saroyan does it often.

How does this differ from the omniscient point of view, since in both cases the story is being told by the author? The author as God is quite different from the author as a person. The author as omniscient voice can tell the reader what everyone is thinking and what is happening everywhere. But the author as person, observer, has bought credibility at the price of omniscience. He may convince us with his "eyewitness" tone, and we may believe he is sensitive and talented enough to be a good observer, but he no longer knows everything. (This tradeoff is demanded again and again in art. You make a decision to gain an effect, but always at a price, the loss of something else. You must weigh carefully to make sure the gain is worth the loss.)

Perhaps the first person point of view narrator isn't even the author anymore, but one of the characters in the story. Wuthering Heights is narrated by Mr. Lockwood, a new neighbor of the mysterious Heathcliff. Some of Conrad's stories are narrated by a character named Marlowe. Willa Cather's My Antonia is narrated by Jim Burden, introduced by Gather as an old friend she grew up with "... in the same Nebraska town .... " Gather quotes her fictitious friend Burden as saying, "I didn't take time to arrange it... I suppose it hasn't any form ...."

With this little trick Cather is saying that the story is written artlessly, not by a writer, but by an ordinary person who feels deeply about some memories. So she gains more authenticity, perhaps at the price of a certain range, since an "ordinary person" might not describe all events with the perception of the writer. In My Antonia this loss is more than compensated for by the dimension Gather adds in the contrast between the rather intellectual yet romantic Jim Burden and the strong, earthy Antonia. The wistful attraction he feels for a girl too different from him perhaps suggests Cather's own longings for the Nebraska plains she had to leave in order to become a great writer about them.

Samuel Butler made a brilliant point of view decision for The Way or All Flesh, which is the story of the birth, growth and coming to manhood of Ernest, told by an old family friend, Mr. Overton.

Actually this is an autobiographical novel, with both Ernest and Overton representing parts of the author, Samuel Butler young and old Samuel Butler viewing the anguish of his youth with the broad understanding and humor of his old age. The voice of Overton (supposedly a writer of comic drama) is even able to comment like omniscient author while maintaining the identity of close friend and eye witness.

The writer gets ultimate authenticity if the "I" of the first person point of view narrator is central in the story. It happened to me! Like Jane Eyre or Moll Flanders ... or far too many of the novels being written today. Of course, no reader thought Sane Eyre was autobiographical, since Bronte used a male pen name and kept her real identity secret for quite a while. And everyone knew Defoe wrote Moll Flanders even though he tacked on a preface saying he was doing oral history. Still, the story gained intensity, as if grabbing reader identification, making the I of the story into the I of the reader. Note that in both examples this intensity is gained at a further withdrawal of the author's presence, and a further loss orange. Jane is a young girl, observant but inexperienced, and Moll is vastly experienced but unlettered and unsubtle. In both cases the reader is expected to be more sophisticated than the narrator, quite difference from the relation between the reader and the omniscient author. In a way, the reader actually participates in the writing by filling in things implied by the action, things the omniscient narrator might tell, but the limited, first person narrator probably doesn't even know.

Ella Price's journal is written from a first person point of view in the voice of a woman who is changing rapidly but is always a step or two behind the reader. She is being changed, not only by her experiences but by the very fact that she is writing them down, experiencing them on paper and rethinking them. The novel works if the reader continues to sympathize with Ella while knowing she cannot always be trusted as a narrator; she must write what she thinks she ought to feel before she can reject it and discover what she really does feel and think. (When readers mistake me for Eland think the book is my journal, I am both glad that I achieved authenticity and impatient that they don't realize how hard it waste get that effect.)

These devices may begin to seem like playing tricks on the reader when he confronts stories told by narrators he can't trust. Henry James' *Turn of the Screw* still keeps readers arguing about whether the governess really saw ghosts or a projection of her own sex obsessions or both, and James' assertion that he meant there were ghosts didn't settle anything. Ring Lardner's story "Haircut' narrated by a friendly, talkative barber. Only gradually does the reader see that the narrator is a cruel, insensitive member of community which has done its best to destroy a couple of vulnerable people. By the end of the story, the reader despises the narrator and sees the truth through his lies.

I wouldn't recommend using such an unpleasant narrator to novel because few readers want to read a whole book written ii voice they despise. I've lost a lot of readers in the first few pages of *Kin of Ata*. My first person narrator starts out as such a tote unsympathetic character that many readers are unwilling to wait signs of improvement in him. I chose him as narrator, first, because needed total first person authenticity to draw the reader into fantasy, and second, because the story needed the abrasion of personality. I had read somewhere that Utopian fantasies became boring because the visiting stranger narrator ended up just ask questions and having philosophical dialogues. I avoided that pit by making my narrator antagonistic, even dangerous to the scene he was describing. I bought authenticity and suspense, but at price of annoying my readers, at the risk of turning some readers away. Shouldn't I have reversed that decision, tried something else. No, because halfway through the first draft I had begun to see the spiritual growth of the narrator was a central theme: the state of his change formed the hidden structure holding the story together. My point of view choice had come from a third deeper reason than those I knew when I made it.

Third person point of view is not much different from first person; All it means is that the writer calls the perceiver of the action she instead of I, but still sees the action through that one person's eyes, perceiving it with that one person's capabilities. This weakens intensity by saying "she" instead of "I" but has a vocabulary advantage over first person point of view, can use richer text that might not be credible in the point of view character's voice. In this way the author may be more "present" if not orprescient.

For example, take a story told from the point of view of a small child. In first person it might read like this:

I saw Mommy fall. She looked funny. She didn't move. I cried and cried and poked her too. But she wouldn't move. In third person the same description could be written like this: Jane watched her mother turning, lurching, looking puzzled as she crumpled to the floor. Jane ran to her laughing.

Was it a game? She pulled at her arm, her sleeve, finally at her hair. Surely now she would move, jump up, even scold Jane. But she did not move, and after a while Jane crumpled too, nestling close to her mother, sobbing. Which version you prefer depends on your general intent, what effect you want to get with whatever leads up to and away from this scene.

The author's voice or ability to paint scenes can operate more expansively in third person narrative, but it need not necessarily. There is a major tradition of sparse third person narrative usually influenced by Hemingway, who often wrote in third person point of view but in a prose stripped bare, devoid of all but the most simple adjectives and called "objective," achieving a tone of tightlipped confrontation with events of deepest significance, evoking deep feelings, by implication more profound than any of the words we have to express them. Sometimes the author writing in this tradition withdraws even from the mind of the central character, leaving us with no point of view figure, but only an objective narrator, a camera which clicks with seeming indifference, leaving the reader to make what she will of the pictures. This method is, of course, not indifferent. Like a photographer, the author arranges people and shoots from angles carefully planned to achieve a specific effect. Walter Van Tilburg Clark once pointed out that this spare, tight lipped narration was most effective when the story happened at the extremes of life and death events, but didn't do much for the broad array of situations and feelings which lay short of the extremes.

Third person narration is hard for me. I usually end up in first person, imitating the voice of one of the characters. But I almost always start out trying to do a novel or story in third person, wishing to claim the range of that broader vocabulary.

I wrote the first draft of Miss Ciardino in third person, even stepping in as omniscient author from time to time, explaining what various characters were doing and thinking. It didn't work, so I cut the parts where I intruded as author, distracting the reader with adding much. It still didn't work. My heroine was an angry person surviving a life of struggle, but in my narration that struggle taken on a tone that seemed a bit relentless. I wanted to keep intensity of her struggle; that was the whole story. Still, I needed some variation in tone.

Then it occurred to me that if I put her memory flashbacks first person present tense, I would keep the intensity I wanted would vary the tone. As I worked, I realized that my alternating between third person past tense (for the ongoing action) and person present tense (for her flashbacks) actually portrayed state: she is a split person, cut off from her feelings, even from her past, by the force of her anger. As memory gradually reveals connects her feelings to her, this alternating pattern occurs less frequently, until the book ends in third person with Giardino's past assimilated and transcended in her final words.

The novel I'm working on now I tried many different ways be I gave in and started using first person. I was trying to avoid the story from the point of view of a person who is not only in immature but blind. Talk about creating problems for myself! (Re Frost once said that writing free verse was like trying to play tennis without a net. However, I think he would have cautioned setting up mile-high nets.) This novel is shaping up much like others in that one of its central themes is the inner growth of the narrator achieved through the process of experiencing and thin and telling the story. This recurring theme may explain why, most of the time, I must use first person point of view.

It was Henry James who showed us that point of view ca more than a device to achieve a certain effect or tone, who could go deeper into the story, into the very theme itself. He story as perception, that the main drama, the main action should be what goes on in a character's head as he or she begins to see, to understand. This growth of understanding became of predominant value for him and he wrote about point of view the central decision which determined what the story really needed.

The most famous example of James' refinement of point of view story is his novel The Ambassadors, written from a single person point of view, that of Strether, an aging man who has I sent to Europe to tell young Chad that it's time to stop sowing give up his mistress, and come home to work in the family business. Strether is in the midst of his own middle age crisis, feeling that he has missed much of life. Entranced by Paris, by Chad's mistress, by everything, he changes sides, defends the lovers and tries to protect them. Nothing is what it seemed to be when he left America. He has learned, broadened, begun to see... however, various doubts begin to creep in, Strether's identification with the lovers begins to creak, and finally he learns that, unfortunately for all his illusions, things were as they originally seemed. Chad is no sensitive young Strether that might have been, but a conventional young man who is tired of his mistress and looking forward to going home to try his hand at the advertising business.

Clearly, the story consists of what goes on in Strether's head. Without his dreams, his wistful longings, his projection of his own needs on what he sees, his changes of perception, his growth in understanding, there is no story. (Or there is a different one if, let us say, it is told from the point of view of Chad's mistress.) Point of view has determined, has become both story and theme.

To achieve that fusion, James stayed in a single point of view throughout this and most of his other novels. Other novelists, after James, continued to shift point of view from one chapter to another, and a few even continue to step in directly as author, omnisciently commenting on the action. But the trend since James has been toward a single, often first person point of view, and toward the total withdrawal of the author.

Aldous Huxley called contemporary writers "squeamish" about taking a central position of authority as storyteller. Sometimes I think that future literary historians will see the single point of view as a quaint mannerism which limits twentieth century literature in the same way that squeamish euphemism in writing about sexual relations limited nineteenth century literature.

For it seems to me that many point of view choices today are not made with James' keen sense of point of view supporting, even comprising theme. They are not choices at all, but mere habit. They are also evasion. Many novels are written from a single point of view (most often first person) not because the material demands it but because the writer can thus evade responsibility for really knowing what the story is all about, what it means.

This irresponsibility and blind following of convention are supported by editors and teachers who recite a rigid dogma made up of an unlikely combination of James and Hemingway. They remind of another incident from my music student days, the time my true Jake, having mastered the elementary rules of traditional harmony based on what Bach did, tried to apply them to Debussy, then announced that Debussy was no good because he wrote parallel fit and octaves. Too many editors, teachers and writing students like Jake. They flinch at point of view shifts from one chapter another, frowning and telling you that such things ... well, they j aren't done much anymore. As for a point of view switch right in middle of the page, jumping from John's mind as he spoke ii Mary's mind as she heard him . .. horrors! And if you come flat in, addressing the reader with some philosophical statement about what these people are doing, your critics may tell you to "stop editorializing and get on with the story."

And the trouble is, most of the time they're right: it didn't quite work. We seem, most of us twentieth century writers, to have I scope, to have lost the ability to move about freely as Tolstoy c or Thackeray or Hardy or Austen. Critics write all kinds of philosophical explanations for this loss: the powerlessness, impotent alienation of modern man reflected in the interior, limited point view, etc. Maybe. But I think we lost range through lack of use.' traded omniscience for other effects. The only way to get it bad by trying it again, probably in a different form. That means defy the authorities who tell you it isn't done by good writers.

E. M. Forster reacted against all these authorities and said ahead and shift point of view; it's all right if it works, if it doesn't the reader. I agree. I can't see anything jarring, for instance, something like this:

John watched Mary gazing through the window at the snow and imagined she was still grieving, longing for the warmth of her San Diego beach house.

Actually Mary's eyes were fixed on the red car parked across the street, the one which had followed her to the bank and all the shops that afternoon.

You'll find better examples of shifts in Virginia Woolf's *Mrs. Logway,* in F. Scott Fitzgerald's *Tender is the Night,* in May Sartc *Birth of a Grandfather,* in James Schevill's *The Arena of Ants,* and strong, responsibly omniscient voice in the works of Doris Lessi.

Examples abound, as soon as you begin looking for them. Study them, learn the devices (including the simple gap on the page!) for making clear and smooth shifts, the way composers of music study and learn traditional cadences which will get them from one key to another totally unrelated key, before they invent their own cadences.

I made an abrupt point of view shift at the beginning of the last chapter of Miss Ciardino. After nearly an entire book told from her point of view, she is suddenly absent while my objective narrative voice records friends talking about her for a few pages. Then I bring her in again, jump back into her head and finish the story from her point of view. I made this shift in order to heighten a final bit of suspense, and I guess it worked because no one seems to have noticed. Readers won't, Forster says, if the story continues to interest them.

So don't be intimidated by everything I've written on this subject or by anyone who says you just can't shift point of view and mustn't editorialize. Try anything. If it doesn't work (and it probably won't at first) change it. But never make a planning decision based on any "rules." Let the rules grow out of the demands of the work, the novel itself.

16. For whom do you not write?

Is this some kind of joke? Unfortunately, no. Some writers aren't even aware that the answer to this question is part of planning. Often they answer the question, make a decision fatal to their book, without knowing they have made any decision at all. A few examples may help to clarify the question, to make you fully aware that it exists.

A writer described to me some hilarious, weird, vicious intrigues within the feminist organization she belongs to, and I suggested that she had great material for a satirical novel. "Oh, I couldn't," she said. "Feminism is so precarious, that kind of criticism would be an awful blow." She writes and does not write for her women's group.

Another writer has worked for ten years on a novel, agreeing with my suggestion that he expand and color in the necessary political background, but somehow just not doing it. Recently he said to me, "I think I can do it now; I feel freer to criticize the party." He has been writing and not writing all these years for associates in an organization he left twenty years ago.

Several teachers I know have written stiff, "literary" novels which are as far from anything they know and feel as the TV fantasies of the student I mentioned in Section 4, and much duller. They are writing and not writing for the approval of their colleagues at the university.

A woman once said to me, "I'd rather write science fiction, but my son (a writer) says that's crap." Clearly she was writing and not writing for him. The boy who told me gleefully that he was writing a novel that would "just destroy" his family is no less dominated by his family, though he may be working something out.

These people all have real or imaginary censors huddled around them while they write, more insidious and inhibiting than a forbidding presence because these are the censors whose approval these writers crave.

Have you?

Samuel Butler's *Way of All Flesh* tells how the hero Ernest moves toward becoming a writer. This movement is mainly one of casting off, giving up the inhibiting influences of his family, his teachers, his friends, his social class. Throughout his awkward, fumbling journey toward himself, there is one friend he continues to admire. Towneley is rich, handsome, funny, generous, poised, honest, charming and beloved by all. Yet as Ernest finds his vocation, he decides to break off with Towneley because, "Towneley is my notion of everything I should most like to be ... I should be in perpetual fear of losing his good opinion if I said things he did not like . . . . "

This story has nothing to do with giving up your friends. It has to do with making sure that you, and not they, write your books. It has to do with making sure that you don't censor or stilt your work to conform to the real or imagined expectations of other people. It has to do with being free to write what you can.

Once you have decided whom you don't write for, can you decide whom you do write for? That's almost harder. Saint Augustine wrote his autobiography to and for God. That's rather a formidable audience. Of course, we all write as an offering to universal consciousness, as the juggler in the legend juggled before the altar (scandalizing the staid worshippers) because that was the best he had to offer. But we need a less awesome consciousness as direct reader.

I used to tell my students to imagine they were writing for a reader like themselves at their best: someone fairly open minded, able to suspend disbelief enough to get into any good book; an attentive reader but not too literary; adventuresome rather than knowledgeable; unassuming, but with instinctive good taste.

I'm not quite sure whom I write for: someone patient enough to go on this exploration with me. But I'm very much on guard against those whom I don't write for, because they always pop into my consciousness when I'm about to say something important, something truer than I thought I knew, and something they might say I ought not to think.

17. Know when to quit.

It's fun scribbling notes on cards, hanging charts on the wall, doing research at your local coffee house. Easier than writing. There's a temptation to go on planning long after the outlines of the book are fairly clear in your mind. We all know people who have been planning a novel for years. It sounds better and better as they develop the plan and tell us about it, much better than the pedestrian things we are plodding through. But I'll bet it won't ever get written.

There comes a time when planning is just an evasion, when you have to stop it all and plunge into the writing. When is that time? Putting aside the special case of the historical novel requiring years of research, I'd say that the planning stage should take no more than a few weeks. After that, the only good reason for delay is that your child just came down with the flu, or your mother is visiting for a week, or you have to take a trip or work overtime. Remember, if you delay, if you stay too long in the planning stage, you run the risk of losing the drive, the impulse from your seed subject.

Sometimes it is even necessary to cut the planning stage short and plunge into the writing before anything is very clear in your head. If you feel this urgency—the fear that if you don't jump in and start writing, you're going to lose your push—ignore some of the steps I suggested. Obey your impulse and jump in. You can always stop to plan when you temporarily run out of steam. (Some writers swear by the alternating "plunge and plan" system.)

And, yes, sometimes you may have to start without a moment conscious planning, to get your feet wet, to commit yourself, grab hold before it gets away. Do what you must. But never prolong the planning stage just because you're afraid to start writing.

18. "The best laid plans..."

Finally, remember that detailed planning is of great value, b only if you understand that it does not work. By that I mean you cannot expect your careful planning to solve in advance many the problems you will run into while writing, nor help you avoid making changes you must make. It is through the writing itself that you learn what it is you are trying to write. You write some of it, and it's not quite right, but the process of writing sets deep forces motion. (That's why if you miss a day you feel as if getting start' again is like moving mountains.) These deep forces shift you to new place, slightly closer to what you can write. Day by day, as you write, everything keeps shifting and changing under your hand

The plan helps in this process, but only if you are ready to deviate from it as you begin to see your direction more clearly.

This is why most people who think they want to write change their minds when they really get into writing seriously. Living with this uncertainty goes against all our desires for security, stability certainty. It goes against our hopes that we can ever know anything completely or finish it to our satisfaction. For, at the completion a novel, you are different from the person who started it, and he can you be satisfied with this book begun by someone else.

This is risky living. Resisting, rejecting this uncertainty is what ex haunts many people who try to write fiction. The writer who me ages to keep going is the one who can accept the fact that, for writer, nothing works.

Writing the First Draft

19. Writing As Meditation

The first draft is the most exciting, exhilarating and terrifying part of the writing. It is exciting because you are discovering things in yourself you didn't know were there and because even more things come from outside yourself, picked up by intuitive powers you never knew you had. It can also be terrifying because most of the time you are afraid of falling off, losing contact with your story.

When you were planning, you divided, categorized and arranged things. Now you must shift, get back into the mood of receiver, like the state of alert receptivity the mystics call meditation or contemplative prayer. It is this state which mystics universally regard as the highest form of meditation, not a passive trance, but a state of total awareness which is hard to achieve except in short spans of time, under certain conditions, and as a result of years of preparation and work, carefully balancing principles which govern the contemplatives whole life.

If you read the mystics' instructions and advice to aspiring contemplatives, you will be struck by the similarity to what you are trying to do. St. Francois de Sales, for instance: "If the heart wanders or is distracted, bring it back to the point quite gently and replace it tenderly in its Master's presence. And even if you did nothing during the whole of your hour but bring your heart back ... though it went away every time you brought it back, your hour would be very well employed." I can't think of any better advice for dealing with that first awful hour of every writing session. It is like the first hour of hiking or practicing the piano. You can name many other activities like these which only begin to go smoothly after the first hour of "getting into it." I don't know why so many people think writing should be different, should begin with instant inspiration. I don't know why it took me so many years to learn that I should accept the misery of the first hour without whining about it, and to learn that its pains might even be a necessary ingredient in the writing that finally followed.

Sometimes you and the writing become one. It takes off, and you seem only to be taking dictation from some inspired source, writing without effort. This feeling is not an infallible assurance of quality; later you must study the results with the same skeptical eye that the true mystic turns on his occasional visions. V. S. Pritchett wrote in *A Cab At The Door* that he had this "burst of genius" feeling only once, as a boy writing a long, imitative, overblown, bad poem. So feeling good doesn't always mean you're writing well. I mention this, not to spoil the moments when the writing fills you with joy, but to reassure you that the mean, sluggish, doubt filled times may also be productive.

People who meditate or pray find that their period of daily meditation raises the quality of their lives. Writers find the quality of their lives determined by whether or not they have put in their writing time each day, not necessarily by how well the writing went. (In later stages of revision you may even be filled with disgust for the book, usually a sign of fatigue.) Just as the mystic builds her meditation on faith and love, the writer must do her writing on trust.

It is this blind, humble, childlike trust which you must learn to depend on while working on the first draft. You must obey Rake's advice in *Letters To A Young Poet*, to put aside all questions of whether or not you are "good." Like an old gold panning prospector, you must resign yourself to digging up a lot of sand from which you will later patiently wash out a few minute particles of gold ore. Remember that in spite of all the planning you have done, you still don't know what this book is all about. The most vivid vision in your head may come out on paper as a wobbly outline of a few dimly seen people in a vague place doing something. For those first shadowy elements to turn into a novel requires the working of many processes, the first being this trusting voyage of discovery, this taking of dictation, this quiet but attentive search.

Next to prayer, this process most resembles play. It is as hard to learn to play as to pray. Remember what it was like to play? To invent, to explore, to try things, to pretend, to talk sense and non-sense in a totally unselfconscious way? No, I don't think you do. I don't think any of us do, once we are no longer children. We can't become children again and wouldn't want to because as writers we need what we've learned as adults. Now we have to learn another kind of play, a freedom relearned in awareness. I can best express this process by saying that we must replace our lost innocence with humility, not the cringing kind, but the simple, good-humored willingness to make fools of ourselves.

Before they sit down to write, especially when doing the first draft, some writers perform little rituals or recite incantations to help them loosen up and get into this receptive, playful mood. One may just take a walk. I know a man who washes the breakfast dishes. He says the warm water induces a meditative state, starts him thinking about the writing. But his wife can't use this one. She has too leftover conflicts about domestic duties versus writing, so she \ past unmade beds and dirty dishes, reciting a psalm or a poet she heads for the desk. One writer mumbles Thoreau's, "We see but little way if we require to understand what we see," and over for a few minutes before starting to write. Another letter, to help him face the blank page and sneak up on the writing. One woman turns on the television at 8 a.m., just a children are leaving for school and just in time for a half hour program that loosens her up for writing. Another reads a few |: from the letters of Vincent Van Gogh, a sure inspiration for artist. Another does some silent, deep breathing. Several writers told me they put a stack of records on the stereo, to play while they writing, a practice that horrifies me. To each his own.

Just be careful, as you were with planning, that your war ritual or invocation of your muse doesn't start getting longer, becoming a substitute for getting started. For procrastinators I recommend three stern repetitions of a sentence by Cather "Blessed is he who has found his work." Then get at it.

20. Your Writer Versus Your Critic

Our writer is that part of us which exults in the mere express! words, feelings, thoughts, that part of us which loves to speak in the microphone and hear the sound of our voice amplified, even are only saying, "One, two, three, four, testing." It falls in love sudden turns of phrase, with amusing incidents invented 0I spot. It is a child, entranced with color and shape, inventing for holding up its finger painting for admiration by Mama, who will surely say, "Wonderful!"

Our critic is not Mama. The critic is a cool, experienced with very high standards. It loves our writer but not as a parent or lover, rather as a teacher whose duty it is to evaluate, to refine, improve. I always see my critic as a dance teacher watching me attempting my thousandth leap and seeing me land pretty well on my feet, says, "Mmmm ... yes. Now, without that little wiggle this time." My critic is always saying, "Again," and expecting something better.

Now, anyone who is pure writer will not know how to separate the gold from the sand, and will write long-winded, cliché-ridden embarrassments. What is good will be overwhelmed by bubbles and fat and unconscious borrowings from others. What could be refined and rethought will be left in half formed mediocrity and will never rise above the raw, cathartic outpourings which, if unexamined, don't even make good therapy. We all know people who are pure writer. They love to read their work to us. Never shy, they fix us with a glittering eye, like the Ancient Mariner, and insist on sharing their latest outpourings. If we are not wildly enthusiastic in our response, if we make even a tiny suggestion, the pure writer becomes very, very angry and accuses us of being insensitive, reactionary and stupid. (Of course, we're always in danger of getting a stupid reaction from a reader, but that's quite another problem.)

The pure critic, of course, does not write.

Tolstoy said the writer and critic must work together and warned against working late at night when your critic might be asleep. I know a few writers who follow Tolstoy's advice while doing the first draft. They tell me they write a sentence, then examine it and rewrite it and rethink it before they go on to the next. Actually they are combining rough draft writing with rewriting. Most of them follow with further rewriting after the first draft is done. If you are this kind of writer, follow your instincts and shuffle together the separated bits of my advice on first draft writing and rewriting, to make them fit your method.

But his method suits very few writers. Most writers, if they stop to rewrite a sentence in the rough draft, simply get bogged down in problems they're not ready to face yet. Worrying over the choice of the right word, they lose momentum and never manage to finish anything. For them as for most of us, the writer and critic do not work well together on the first draft, but are always pulling at each other. Walter Van Tilburg Clark once wrote a very funny essay about the conflict between his writer and his critic, who stood behind the typewriter constantly shaking her head and saying, "No, no, that won't do!"

During first draft writing I recommend that the critic be put to sleep. Some writers have such a strong critic that it seems almost necessary to bludgeon the damned thing to death in order to stop its nagging and get enough peace and quiet to write the first draft. But you don't want to kill it, just persuade it to go away and do something else for a while. And let you play. It may keep sneaking back into the room and looking over your shoulder, but just tell it again and again to go away and rest because it's going to have plenty of work to do later when you get into rewriting.

If your critic is a real pest, you may want to invent a little sign like the two fingers against the evil eye, or the cross held up before Count Dracula, to drive your critic off. Eventually you should able to get rid of it in a friendly way, so that it doesn't come charming back in at your first sign of fatigue and trample everything you've done. I'm convinced that much of the misery and agony of writing comes from turning this problem into a battle, rather than dealing with it patiently, calmly, and with a sense of humor.

One final word about your critic. When you find your story beginning to deviate from your outline, your characters doing new thing: and everything moving in a direction you had not anticipated, it your critic who will come running in, waving your outline at you. Pay no attention.

21. Pace and Temperament: Flaubert Versus Sand

During the last twelve years of her life, George Sand and Gustav Flaubert carried on a lively correspondence. Sand wrote of her domestic dramas, her political passions, her long walks in the country (exhorting Flaubert to get more exercise) and her night habit, after everyone else was in bed, of writing ten thousand and thirty thousand words. The answers of Flaubert (sedentary, solitary protected from crass contacts by his mama) were sharp thrusts .Sand's idealism and expansive maternal love (he wrote that she had to learn to hate a little). It was in one of these letters that he made his famous complaint about writing: that it took him all day I decide to put in a comma ... and at the end of the day he took out again.

Reading these letters helps us remember the extremes of temperament that can exist in people who are alike in their commitment l writing. For it is chiefly temperament which determines the pace in writing.

Some writers start off in a vigorous rush and don't dare stop writing they've got things moving. One of these "rushers" might isolate herself for many hours, writing until felled by exhaustion, then taking short rest, then plunging in again in pursuit of the story, as if it might get away from her (as indeed it might) if she stops chasing it. She might finish a first draft in a few weeks.

At the other extreme is the writer whose story comes to him in slow drops. This has nothing to do with an inhibiting critic. The writer simply must wait for the mist of his story to gather and condense, to form a drop which eventually falls, plop, on him. Then he must wait for the next drop. For such a writer, the first draft may take many months or even years.

Most of us fall somewhere between these two extremes, leaning a bit toward one or the other, and with slight variation of pace from one book to another. Part of learning to write is learning your natural pace, which is an inherent trait, unchangeable as the color of your hair. You may dye your hair a different color, but not without doing it some damage. You cannot change its true color, which soon reappears at the roots. The damage to your writing can be much more serious, if you try to alter its natural pace, which grows out of your individual temperament. Accepting your own temperament is part of assuming the humble, contemplative mood in which the first draft should be written.

Over the years I have learned that when I am working on the first draft, I cannot work more than three hours a day. Since I'm not a Flaubert, I am tempted to go on, to be a Sand or Dostoevsky, pushing onward while I'm hot. If I do, I only borrow from the next day's work, like being overdrawn at the bank, all credit cancelled till I pay back what I borrowed. In trying to force the flow I only exhaust it. So I seldom write more than one thousand words during these three hours, and if the end of that thousand words comes at a point where I'm just picking up momentum, sliding into a good part that I feel sure of... I stop anyway. Hemingway used to say he stopped when he knew what was coming next, so that he'd be able to get going again the next day. For me, that's good advice; during the first draft writing, I live in constant fear that the flow will suddenly dry up.

But what I've learned about myself is of little use to you. It's up to you to find your own inner rules and accept them. This is more important and more difficult than it seems. Beginning writers are hungry for answers to questions like, what time of day do you work? how fast do you write? do you drink coffee? do you write by hand or at the typewriter? electric or manual? Since details of technique are easy to talk about, we are tempted to hope that they contain the secrets of creativity. But they don't. They are matters of individual temperament, essential for one writer, irrelevant for another. To copy a habit that comes out of someone else's temperament is futile and self-defeating.

Like all people, all writers are different. We do our best work when we can adopt habits which are congenial to our individual temperaments. This doesn't mean we will necessarily enjoy working the way we do. (Flaubert didn't seem to.) It just means we will write as we must.

It also means that if any of the advice in this book doesn't suit your temperament, you must reject it at once and be the kind of writer you are.

22. The Beginning

Am I referring to the beginning of the book or to beginning the writing? Well, both. Getting started can be very hard for people who have trouble with beginnings. After all, where do beginnings begin? How far back in time does anything really start?

Aside from such deep questions, there are simple problems that make beginnings hard. You have to do a lot of things at the beginning of a book: introduce characters; set scenes; get things fixed in the reader's mind so that he can keep track of them; make characters interesting, so that the reader cares about them enough to go on reading; set a particular mood or tone. You may feel that despite your careful planning you don't know your characters well enough yet to be able to do all this right at the start.

You don't have to start at the beginning. You can start at the end if you want to, or anywhere else. That's one of the advantages of having an outline to help you fit all the parts together. F. Scott Fitzgerald recommended starting at a point of tension, a scene you see clearly, vividly, surely, then working your way backward and forward from that point. If beginnings give you trouble, you might find this the best way to get started.

Some writers don't mind beginning at the beginning. They feel pretty certain about their people and places, feel eager to launch them into their story. The most serious question these writers face is how much to tell in the beginning, and how much to leave to be revealed by action and dialogue as the book goes on. You've probably been told that books should start with a bang, with a scene that plunges the characters directly into conflict, grabs the reader and holds her until you can fill in background later. And this advice isn't exemplified only by a detective story with a murder on the first page. The most frequently given example is the highly respected and skillful opening of Anna Karenina:

Everything was in confusion in the Oblongs household.

The wife had found out that the husband had had an affair with their French governess and . .. I agree that's wonderful. But I also love the leisurely opening of Butler's The Way of All Flesh, which begins, "When I was a small boy at the beginning of the century..." and goes on with sixteen (short) chapters describing the antecedents of the hero. That sort of opening is out of style now, but, if it fits your material as well as it did Butler's, try it. Remember, what's out today may be in again by the time you finish the book.

My writing students used to tell me I had one unwritten rule for beginnings: throw out the first three pages (or more). I usually did end up saying something like that, because most beginning writers have trouble telling the difference between necessary introduction and simple warm-up writing. Probably you'll do a lot of warm-up writing at the beginning, parts you'll throw away later. But that doesn't mean warm-ups aren't necessary. Athletes who don't warm up with all that silly jumping up and down tend to break bones when they get into the game. So don't begrudge yourself some warm-up words, don't hold back: there are plenty more where they came from. This advice goes for getting started each day as well as getting started on any particular story.

Remember that the easiest part of rewriting is cutting. You can always trim down what's there, but you have to have something to trim. What's really hard is putting in later something you left out, held back, because each time you insert new material you disturb the rhythm of the whole. So don't be afraid to put in all the details at the beginning.

23. The Middle

If you are a writer who begins at the beginning, your bad timing most likely come when you reach the middle. This is where novels get into trouble, for various reasons.

Let's take the worst possible reason first, the one that first came to you: it won't work. It was a good idea, but you didn't really novel. These people aren't going anywhere. Better forge whole thing. Put it away, and you might be able someday salvage part of it for a short story or use one of the character another novel. Or you might get back to it in a year or two and you've learned enough by then to make it work.

I have a file drawer full of aborted novels from my first ten of writing. There were external reasons why they collapsed in middle, mostly family and teaching responsibilities that tool much energy. But there were internal reasons too. I was learn to write, and it was necessary for me to go through what I did. I saw each unfinished book as a failure, evidence that I was not a "real writer," proof that I ought to quit and put my energy in something "useful."

I know now that every "failed" novel of those years was a necessary in finding my way to the novel I could write. Every novelist, no matter how long he or she has been writing, will have books that die half-finished. The beginner sees them as budding talent, and the experienced writer fears them as a sign of failure powers. In both cases I prefer a more optimistic interpretation writer is attempting a new task, a new challenge, and going as I possible with it, perhaps stopping short of completion, but lea something useful for the next one. We are always setting h, tasks for ourselves, always starting something we're not sure w< finish. That is why every experienced writer I know says, "It harder."

But if you habitually quit in the middle, you may have established a bad pattern simply by misunderstanding the signs. You think you have reached a dead end when all you need to do make a slight detour.

You may just be tired, especially if you lean toward the Sand type who pours it all out as fast as possible. Purely fatigue can feel like depression and the sure conviction that you are not a novelist, not a writer at all... and so on and on. When really means is that you need to take a few days' rest, lay off the coffee and cigarettes, enjoy a long walk or a movie or whatever will rest your brain and exercise your body toward simple physical recovery.

That's the easy solution. A more complicated reason for sagging in the middle is also more exciting: you didn't know what you were getting into and now that you're there, you don't know what to do about it. You've deviated from your outline. New characters you never heard of have suddenly come bouncing in uninvited. This doesn't look anything like the book you thought you meant to write! You're like the woman who said, "How can I know what I think until I hear what I say?"

The solution is simply to keep on saying it, whatever it is. Push on with your new characters doing all these odd new things and see what happens. Doesn't that mean you'll have to go back and change the beginning? Sure, but not now. Not until you begin to re write. That comes later. Keep going, play on. You can fiddle with your outline a bit to help legitimize your deviancy and keep your faith that something inside you knows what it's doing.

There's a much more devastating block that sometimes confronts me when I get to the middle. It's not that I'm tired or that things have gone flying out of control. No, a much more sinister process starts, a gradual slowing down, a nagging feeling that Something Terrible is happening, a slow dying. Then comes what feels like the death of the book, a moment of real despair, full of all the usual implications: I can't write anymore, never could write, this is no good, nothing I ever did was ... and so on.

A few days pass. I brood. Sometimes I talk to my husband or close friend, neither of whom has any idea what I'm working on, and I'm afraid to deliver the coup de gras to my book by telling them, so I just sort of moan and growl vague complaints to them. If no new light comes, no new energy, no answer to What Went Wrong! comes to me in a week or two, I bury the corpse in my file.

No doubt, I tell myself with stern good cheer, I've learned something important which I'll use on the next book.

But sometimes it isn't really a death, not as often as it used to be. When I really reach bottom, real conviction that it's hopeless, I suddenly get a flash, a kind of breakthrough or a glimpse of a new turn writing. What I have to do is to reverse a planning decision, to see a possibility that never occurred to me. Yet, when I see recognize it as if I'd always known it.

Suddenly I see the story as told from a different point of and/or in a different form. I know it will work that way. Desperation comes excitement. Content has shown me its form. I start all again, more scared than ever (because this is a second chance, despair is at least final) with new energy, like a second wind runner. Usually I feel a deeper certainty of having found what the book needs, and it is probably this certainty that releases energy.

Isn't this just the sort of thing I said happens to writers who plan? After all my careful planning, how come it happened?

It's not quite the same, though it resembles what happens ' you don't plan. The trouble definitely came out of a deferred running decision. The question is, could I have made the decision earlier and avoided all this trouble? I don't think so. It has happened often enough that I begin to feel it has something to do with the way my blood flows or with my metabolic rate. I seem to do looks like complete planning, then get into the writing, and have to stop, realizing the real plan, then start again. I'm becoming convinced that every halting step I make, from the first note or last stumbling word before I stop in the middle, has to be made all part of the process. For me. For now.

I tell you all this as a warning not to accept trouble in the first draft as the death of the book, not until you exhausted every possibility of keeping things going. Skip ahead somewhere near the end. (You can fill in the gaps later.) Or going, keep pushing right on through the middle, forcing your characters onward, stampeding them through dreadful antics that know will have to be cut out later; keep them running in rather than let them lie down and die. Or make lists of change; form or content. Or forbid yourself to write or read anything for a solid week of meditating on the problem like Bronte. But don't give up too soon. Do everything you can think of before deciding the mess and forget it. Remember that when you and your have frozen, you may be on the brink of starting the book you are trying to write.

24. The Ending

I usually know just how I'm going to finish a novel. Often I see the last few sentences quite clearly as soon as I have any sense of the novel at all. That doesn't mean I find endings, defined as the last one third or last one fourth of the book, easy. Most endings of novels are unsatisfying and unsatisfactory. Why? Forster thought the writer simply become tired, ran out of energy, made a lot of compromises, and quit. I think there are often other reasons.

One trouble is that endings are so artificial. Fairy tales can end very nicely with "... they were married and lived happily ever after." But in an adult novel you can't get away with such nonsense. The only real ending of a story is the death of all the characters, and we're not quite sure even death is the end, are we? Can't we say that particular episode in the lives of the characters ends at a certain point? Yes and no. Events lead into other events, endings become new beginnings. The novelist has the problem of giving a segment of life that stands complete in itself, though obviously set in the con text of life that goes on. The problem is working toward a place where it makes sense to stop.

Most writers can plunge characters into a situation which seems inevitable for them, but... then what? In real life people often just go on thrashing about in one or another variation of acts dictated by their character, for years and years. This lifelong thrashing becomes unsatisfactory, even boring, in a novel. The shorter forms, the short story or poem, more successfully suggest unchanging, repetitive life patterns without wearying the reader. Or perhaps the comic novelist can make each repetition of the behavior pattern more hilarious than the last. Otherwise, the novelist has to bring about some change that leads toward a satisfying ending for the book.

I had a lot of trouble with the ending of Ella Price's journal. I got Ella opened up to learning, unable to go back to where she was.

Then I put her through the detours of a love affair and a beginning pregnancy, both evasions that she would have to realize were ways of trying to turn back. I knew the book would close with her leaving her husband. But I couldn't figure out how to move from the frozen point where she was trying to turn back, to the final scene where she gathers enough desperate courage to move on. So I tried to bluff it through. I invented new incidents, even new characters, a dizzying

If series of events to keep things moving and to mask the fact didn't know how to get to the place where I could stop through all this action, I finally got to those last few page: sure of from the beginning.

Two years later, given a few sharp words from an editor able to see how, rather than complicating the action, I need focus more sharply on the conflict between Ella and her hi keeping a firm grip on them through some pretty tough see the end. In that time I had gained distance from Ella's story important, I had grown through more writing, thinking, and relating what I'd learned. (That's why you must never sit around and wait for publication before going on to more writing.) The reason that when I went back to rewrite that ending, understood better what my book was about, why it had to finish it and what the ending meant.

By the way, I hated that period of rewriting. I was bored and wanted to get on with other projects. But in those two weeks of drudgery unrelieved by a spark of fun, I made a giant step learning how to take a book to its real completion.

71

I think my experience illustrates the most important with endings in the first draft. They are usually unsatisfactory impossible to arrive at, because the writer doesn't yet understand his own material. He can only come to this understanding t rewriting, rethinking, until he knows more and more about character and their situation. When the writer reaches real knowledge, real insight into his creation, endings take care of themselves.

Most writers, like most other human beings, fall short of understanding. How far short we fall depends on us, on how we are to work and think our way through successive rewrite;

But we're not supposed to be discussing rewriting. We're the first draft. What bit of advice will help now? Just this; make up your mind about anything. Once you have survived the middle and are pushing on through the ending, you will find there are probably loose ends, even new threads, hanging over the place. Let them hang, develop them further if they be developed. Don't be tempted to trim off rough edges and everything to the neat close you listed on your outline. Different person now from the person who wrote that out there may be some new and different elements that you're too tired to see clearly. After a rest restores your energy, you'll go back to work with heightened intelligence, ready to make more discoveries of what you've been trying to do, with more understanding of what can be done.

25. "Don't save anything'

That's all Willa Gather said when she was asked if she had any advice for young writers.

"Don't save anything." If new things come during the first draft writing, new characters, new actions, dialogue that takes the whole thing off in a new direction, don't hold back. Let it happen, pour it all out, follow where it leads.

"Don't save anything." If you start hearing and seeing things in your daily life that seem to want to bypass your journal and go directly into this first draft, let them in. One uncanny experience you'll have while writing a novel is that when all your faculties become fixed on your project, things start happening as if staged for your benefit. Bits of dialogue and models for characters start appearing. Use them.

"Don't save anything!" Put everything you've got into the rough draft of this one book, as if it's the only book you'll ever write. Put in all the movement and passion and emotion you see, ail the know ledge you have of how people think and act. I don't mean to make a hodgepodge of every idea that ever occurred to you. Within the scope of what this novel of yours can do, put in everything you know, everything, so that by the end of the rough draft, you feel as if you have said everything you'll ever have to say, are empty, and done.

Maybe you are. Maybe you are "the man of one book." If that's true, at least you'll have made your one book as rich as it can be. More likely, however, you will find that in the process of giving "everything" to this one book, you have cleared space and channels for the inrush of new material for the next book, along with new strength and skill to shape it.

Revising

26. "Writing is rewriting"

Robert Frost said his famous "Stopping by Woods on a Snow' Evening" came to him spontaneously, as if dictated, fully formed written out in a few minutes and never revised. I have heard similar accounts of the creation of some short stories and even, occasionally, of a novel. It is possible. Even allowing for the fact that writer often tell tall tales about the process of writing, it is possible. Even remembering that the inspired, perfect work usually comes "spontaneously" after years of daily uninspired work, like the basketball player's perfect toss that came after thousands of tries, I do believe a novel could be written that would require almost no revision. But not often.

"Writing is rewriting." I don't know who first said that. Everyone, guess. Everyone who's ever seriously tried to write says it sooner c later.

Writers are fond of comparing the writing of a novel to the gestation and birth of a child. Men especially like to write about the agonizing labor of giving birth to a book. That's okay. The only thing wrong with the metaphor is that is not carried far enough. The planning stages are rather like a pregnancy, and the writing the first draft is like the labor of childbirth: intense, joyful, exciting; painful and exhausting.

But finishing the book, bringing it through rewriting to compilation, is more like raising the born child to adulthood: a long, time-consuming, often tedious and exasperating job which requires more patience and devotion than we thought we were capable of. Conceiving and giving birth does not make a woman a mother. Mother is the person who, after birth, puts in those long, caring years. Finishing a first draft doesn't make you a novelist. Anyone can do the rough draft of a novel, and it probably won't look much worse than the first draft of any great novel you care to name. The difference between "anyone" and a serious writer is rewriting, rewriting, and more rewriting, sometimes over a period of years.

This may be a discouraging enough prospect to make most beginners decide to quit. But the serious novelist reads these words with cautious yet growing elation. "Do you mean that the first draft of_____ (fill in the title of your favorite great novel) looked as bad as mine does?" Probably. "Does that mean that if I rewrite and rethink and rewrite, I can write a novel, good as that?" Possibly. Not likely. But possibly. For the serious writer those cautious words open up the heavens. For if a good novel doesn't spring into life by some mysterious miracle ... if it wasn't written in a burst of genius, in an ecstatic trance...

It is at this point that we serious writers remember Einstein's "Genius is the infinite capacity for taking pains" and, grinning over our gritted teeth, decide that we can work as hard as anyone.

27. First, Set it cool.

It used to be the almost universal, worldwide custom (and still is in some cultures) that after the birth of a baby the mother was exempted from all duties, except nursing her baby, for six weeks. She was waited on, pampered, indulged and encouraged to be irresponsible and lazy. My grandmother used to shake her head at the way modern mothers leaped back into normal activities. She wasn't at all surprised when one of them became depressed and irritable a few months later. "You can't go against Nature," she would say. "Six weeks rest."

The same period of time seems to be the minimum rest period fora manuscript: six weeks or more in which you don't write in it, reedit, or if possible even think about it. One reason for this layoff is that you need to get distance from it. You must get out, clean up some space for your critic to work. You should aim to get so far away from it that when you look at it again, it will seem almost as if you're reading the work of someone else.

The second reason for a layoff is that physically and spiritually you are empty, exhausted. Before you can get back to the work of

75

rewriting your infant book, you need a period of recovery. If you start rewriting too soon, you'll be going on your nerves and may end up in post partook depression and disorientation, of little use to yourself or your book. You need some pampering, rest, freedom.

You need a change.

What kind of a change?

Ideally you'd spend a couple of days sitting in the sun talking with warm, intelligent friends, followed by a few weeks of comfortable travel (arranged by someone else) alone or with your favorite relatives and friends. Then ... but you can go on filling in this dream.

Lacking the money or the time for such an idyll, most of us ha to make do with other changes. Probably you will find that you' let so many things go that catching up with the rest of your life v provide plenty of change: getting reacquainted with your family and friends, catching up on domestic chores, tackling the back of work at your job, reading. (Some writers find it hard to read when working on a novel.)

Adventures are even more conducive to recovery, so try to something different: a walk you've never taken before, a trip to t zoo, an art exhibit, or any place that's off your usual rounds. During one period of my life, when I was broke and busy with job and I could take only an hour or so at a time for "adventures" t\ would speed recovery. So I answered want ads: "Antiques for sale' or "Apartment for rent," (in a part of town I hardly knew) "Moving, selling record collection." (That one turned out to be Persian trapeze artist who was going to Africa on tour. He serve me a cup of tea while we listened to some records, and we had long talk about the decline of the circus in America.) Answering took me, at no cost, into unfamiliar settings and occasionally in situations almost as foreign as those I might encounter on a trip.

If you are a compulsive writer like me, you may find that to weeks of no writing is the absolute maximum before a case of hi anxiety threatens to wipe out the rest and change benefits. The answer is to write something else, a short story, a review (Virginia Woolf rested by doing some of the best critical writing we have long journal entries, letters to neglected friends, a few notes books you plan for the future, anything, as long as you don't tour The Novel until you are, as an editor once put it, "well rinsed."

Sometimes a totally different experience, like a trip, will short the recovery time. Last year I knew I had to make a one week trip the east coast. I managed to time things so that I finished the final draft of a novel before I left. For one week I rushed around unfamiliar places meeting unfamiliar people. Then home, and with and week to put myself together and catch up on chores, I felt ready begin the first rewrite.

If you have a family and a job, you will find that it is impossible to write during certain periods like Christmas holidays or invented days at work. There is no escape from these enforced layoffs, which are all the more exasperating because they're nobody's fault. But one way of living with them is to schedule rewriting stints around them, using them as rest and change periods.

Am I seriously suggesting that artistic inspiration can be put on a schedule? Well ... uh ... yes, sometimes it can, especially if the only alternative is letting it wither away.

28. Read it through.

Now it's time to wake up the critic in you, who will read the manuscript with strict attention and high standards, understanding that this is not your final, finished effort. I always read the whole thing through fairly quickly before I choose what to start working on. This is no time to get bogged down in correcting the spelling. What I want is a general sense of how it moves and where it doesn't. As I read I make little penciled notes in the margin to remind me of my initial reaction as reader critic. Often these notes are in the form of questions: Would she have said it that way? Cut this? Credible? Introduce sooner?

Gradually or suddenly I become aware of parts that don't fit together, of huge gaps where something is needed to connect things up. I may put in an extra sheet of paper on which I outline these bigger problems. In the second part of the book, I will find things not prepared for in the first part, or I may find that something I started in the first part was allowed to fade away later. I make notes on everything, surveying the manuscript like a policeman at the site of a collision. I try to list the damages coolly, in the cop's mood of alert but routine investigation, though part of me feels like the driver who caused the accident, standing there in the midst of broken glass, partly in shock, partly furious at my wrong turning.

Too often we think of criticism as purely negative, telling us only what's wrong. Or we think of the critic as passing down a sweeping verdict on the whole book: good or bad. That's because we read "good" or "bad" reviews which hand down a verdict based on careless reading or ignorant bias. These reviews are not written by critics.

The rare, real critic is generous. She will unerringly spot a weakness, but she delights in finding strength, celebrating good writing and praying for its increase. You must be that rare, complete critic, identifying all the weak spots but paying special attention to the strong ones.

As you read through your first draft, you will come to places where your eye skims along, you forget you are reading, and you enter the world of the book not because your critic has fallen asleep again, but because it is living the story, absorbed by good writing. These are the parts that work! Maybe for a couple of pages. Maybe for only a couple of lines. But they take you in, they live, and you know that these parts can stand as they are. What you have to do is to make the rest of the book come up to them. You examine these good parts and wonder how you did them; you can't remember! Sometimes, you can't even remember having written them.

Examining the "good parts" may give you mixed feelings of elation and despair, since you wonder how you can make good writing happen by any conscious effort. But you should pay some attention, show respect, because these good parts are the keys to what you do well. They are the signposts that point you in the right direction toward developing your voice, your style.

I don't often use the word style because most beginning writers think of style as some kind of elegance or grace. They must impose on the material they work with. Your style is just you. You cannot learn or copy it from someone else. You cannot invent it out of nothing. You can only discover it, recognizing it first in these occasional "good parts," then nourishing it and helping it grow.

I don't mean that when you do something well, you should keep doing it over and over, never trying a new challenge. Your style is deeper than that; it is your special strength that supports your attempts to do many things. Sometimes we writers find it hard to value our own strength. What we're good at may seem too easy. Sometimes we wish we could write like someone else we admire, and that desire may make us blind to what we can do well. Accepting whatever it is you do well, and trying to learn to do it better and better, means the same thing as accepting yourself, and that seems to be as hard for writers to do as for anyone else.

29. Making Changes

What do you do first? Overhaul the third chapter? Change that word? Redo that character in the beginning, to match what she became in the middle? Give the central character two children instead of three, and which one should you wipe out? Cut out that whole scene? Take out that comma? Put it back in?

When I think of the process of working over a manuscript, I think of my father, who has been a natural mechanic from the time he was big enough to hold a wrench. He made our living fixing cars, but he could fix anything. He used to bring home power tools left at the local dump and tinker with them until he got them running again. All the kids in the neighborhood brought their bikes for him to fix. Long after I left home, I was always bringing him my car and every small appliance that broke down, with total faith that, "Pop will fix it."

He would take a strange machine apart and silently contemplate it for a while. Then would come a series of grunts and mumbles, to himself and to the machine, as he began to tinker with it. He tried this and that, never in a hurry, rearranging parts, improvising new parts from the wires, washers and other bits and pieces stored in boxes in his garage. Then, after minutes, hours, or days, he would bring it to me, smile, and say, "Now try it." And, of course, it worked perfectly, even better than before, since he had probably oiled and cleaned it as well. When he explained what was wrong and how head fixed it, I understood little of what he told me, but I realized that his skill was part of his loving fascination with the way machines work, his enjoyment of tinkering with all the parts, patiently exploring, discovering.

Good rewriting demands this kind of easy, unhurried tinkering with words. This purposeful yet relaxed tinkering demands a certain kind of faith that it can be done successfully. My father never doubted his ability to understand and repair anything that had been designed and made by another human being. He knew that with enough patience he'd succeed. As writers we're trying to make something different from what another human being has made, yet we must keep a similar faith: since we created the problem, it is likely that we can find the solution. I know this isn't always true, but it is true more often than we think. I know that if I sit down or walk around or go to sleep with a rewriting problem, believing that the solution will come, chances are it will. Not always on the first try. But each unsuccessful try eliminates another wrong solution and leads me to the right one. I can't emphasize too strongly how important this is, the fact that writing leads to writing, that failed attempts lead to eventual success, that the solution to a rewriting problem is made up of all the attempts that led nowhere.

The trouble is that when you're just beginning to write, you may feel that words committed to paper are sacred, fixed, immutable, and that things that do not work are forever failures. But you're not dealing with a finished, printed, copyrighted book, only with an idea of one, a pile of words that will change many times before they take shape as a book.

All you need are patience, a pair of scissors, and a roll of scotch tape. (Or better yet, use a computer!) Yes, at last I can give you one definite, universal rule for writing. Ready? Don't make additions and changes in the margin or on the back of the page. Cut and splice, rather than scribble and squeeze in, your changes. This method prolongs the time you can work on this version, before you have to type a clean copy just to be able to see what you are doing.

Start wherever you can, fixing up a little thing first, perhaps, to give you courage to tackle a big one. Then fix up whatever you disturbed by fixing, because rewriting leads to more rewriting. It re minds me of my days as a music student, when we did harmony exercises, putting in the chords under a melody according to strict rules. When I found I had committed forbidden parallel fifths, I changed the voice leading, only to find that one change altered the relation of all the parts, leading to more and more changes. The difference between harmony exercises and your writing is that in your writing, the rules are not imposed from without, but grow from the material itself and gradually reveal themselves in the rewriting.

I wish I could give you an authentic sample of my own rewriting, step by step, but I doubt that I could ever salvage the real thing. Those facsimiles you sometimes see of a famous writer's manuscript, with scribbled corrections, don't begin to show the think scribble retype patch-up process as it really takes place. Out ofcuriosity I once tried to keep every version of one short story, to keep track of its formation. But I gave up when I found myself getting lost in a mass of tattered scraps. I'm puzzled when I hear writers say they keep working manuscripts for collectors' archives; if I did, I'd soon be buried under a mountain of paper.

However, I did keep the rough first draft manuscript of Miss Ciardino, so I can offer you a sample from that. And, while I can't show the stages it passed through, I'll try to recall some of them and explain how it became the final version.

"Then let me ask you one more question," said Maria.

"Does it help if I tell you that you were the best teacher I ever had? If I say, in spite of what happened between us, I learned more from you than from anyone, that I found myself using methods I learned in your class, and that they're still good. Does it help, in your feeling about Camino and all those years, when I tell you that?"

Anna smiled, then took a deep breath. "A little, but... "

She shook her head slowly. "No, it doesn't really touch anything deep, it doesn't change anything, if that's what you mean."

"That's what I was afraid you'd say," said Maria. "That's why I ... tell me, why didn't you leave teaching?"

"Leave teaching?" Anna looked at Maria without comprehension. "I can't imagine doing anything else. Teaching was what I did well. It was my work. From the first moment

I walked into a classroom, when I was a child, I knew that was where I belonged."

"You can say that, and at the same time think about what it did, what teaching does to your life?"

Now Anna felt very impatient. "It is quite possible toehold in the mind two ideas which cannot be reconciled.

81

One: I have hated teaching more than I loved it. It has hurt me and taken much from me and given back little. Two:

It is my work. It is what I do. If I were to live my life again,

I would have to be a teacher again." She said it as though pronouncing sentence on herself. She could see the slight shake of Maria's head that showed her retreat from this.

She pointed her finger at Maria, in the same way she had often pressed an important point in the classroom, drilling it into them whether they liked it or not. "Take care how you reject an idea that doesn't please you. That's how you stop thinking, and once you stop thinking, you stop being human."

Maria surprised her by laughing. "Oh, I used to love it when you stood in front of the class that way. It was frightening but thrilling too."

Anna dropped her hand into her lap. She felt ridiculous.

"I guess I've tired you," said Maria.

Anna shook her head. "You've just reminded me of many things, many more things. You see, I keep trying to remember what happened to me the other night. It is blacked out, blocked. But I keep remembering things from years ago.

Things I'd rather not remember. Those are the things that tire me."

"Sorry," said Maria. "We were going to talk about your... injury, and we went all around again and back to teaching."

Anna laughed. "That's what Arnold... an old friend of mine... used to complain of. He said you couldn't have two teachers in a crowded room without the conversation turning to teaching ... that teachers could talk about nothing else."

Maria stood up. "I've got to go... pick up my son at nursery school."

"I'm glad to have seen you again, Maria." Anna stood, took her hand and shook it. "No matter what I said ... it meant a good deal to me, this visit. I'm only sorry that I wasn't able to be of more help in talking to you about your problems."

Their eyes were on a level now and Maria looked into hers steadily as she said, "Miss Giordano, I've never spoken to you without learning something."

Clearly, there is a lot of fat to be trimmed from this. The first thing I got rid of, as I remember, was Anna's speech about her hate love relation to teaching. That was implied everywhere in the bookend could be adequately summed up by a simple, "Teaching was my work." I threw out the reference to Arnold's statement, which also was intrinsic to the book. Then I got rid of Anna's reference to the mysterious incident she was trying to remember. I had already sprinkled enough references to it throughout the book.

All those things could be cut, but remember, I couldn't decide to cut them until I had viewed the entire book several times while revising. That's why I urge you not to "save anything" and not to worry about repetition in the first draft. If you have several statements of the same thing, you can save the ones that work, lopping off the others without, usually, even leaving a sign that they were ever there.

It was a harder decision to get rid of Anna's fingerprinting gesture. I loved that part. I could just see her doing it, and I loved defusing it with Maria's delighted laugh. But I finally had to conclude that there were too many statements of Anna's austerity. If the reader were to be able to sympathize with her, and if Anna were not to sink into stereotype, some of these gestures would have to go.

Along with these cuts I did the usual cleanup work, correcting my grammar and spelling, sharpening diction. So is my rewriting just cutting and cleaning? No, not just.

After redoing this scene a few times, and after working on the end of the book, I began to feel that Miss Giardino's final decision about her life carried her austerity too far. I had left her too much alone at the end. It was in character for her to choose the hard, independent, austere way, but it was not in keeping with her change that she should drop back into the isolation she had suffered for several years. So I went back into other scenes, adding a few more letters received from former students. In the final scene I spread these letters out on a table where Anna was seated, answering them, a hint of renewed contacts with people. Then I added her mention of a dinner date with Maria, hinting that the young former student might become her friend. To support this, I had to go back to the earlier scene between them, adding a hint of future contact between them, with Maria's statement that she wants to see Anna again. This statement also added some warmth to

Anna, indicating Maria not only respected her but liked her. The fact that Anna seems surprised at this possibility made her, I hoped, even more likeable. So here's the final version:

"Then let me ask you one more question," said Maria. "Does it help if I tell you that you were the best teacher I ever had? If I say, in spite of what happened between us, I learned more from you than from anyone else, that I use methods I learned in your class, and they're still good. Does it help, in your feeling about Camino and all those years, when I tell you that?"

Anna smiled and took a deep breath while she thought. "I'd like to say that makes it all worthwhile. But..." She shrugged. Did knowing you were in the right help after the car had run over you?

"Then I just can't understand why you didn't leave teaching." Anna hesitated, almost stammering at such a strange question. "Teaching was my work."

Maria waited as if Anna must have more to say. But what else was there to say? Finally Maria stood. "I have to pick up my son at nursery school."

"I'm glad you came, Maria." Anna stood and extended her hand. Their handshake was firm, as if sealing an agreement. "No matter what I said, it meant a great deal to me, your visit. I'm only sorry that I wasn't able to be of more help, to tell you something useful."

Maria look steadily into Anna's eyes as she said, "Miss Giordano, I've never spoken to you without learning something. May I come again?"

Anna was surprised. "Why, yes. If you really want to."

"I really want to."

And now as I look at that scene, I see a place where ... but no I'm done with it. It must stand as it is.

Rewriting is tedious, especially if you are doing it well. You will miss the excitement of writing the first draft. The exhilaration and spontaneity are gone. But so is the tension, the fear that you'll lose it, abort the novel before you're halfway into it. This means there': less drain of energy in rewriting, and you may find you can work to longer periods without anxiety, without feeling your nerve: stretched out like rubber bands at the snapping point. Interruption: won't bother you as much, nor will working for short periods more than once a day (if necessary because of other demands on you rather than the longer sessions of first draft writing. Often, in re writing, you'll find the solution to a problem while you're doing something else, not even thinking about the book, and you can make a note of it and do the change whenever it's convenient, with no danger of losing impetus or inspiration.

Rewriting involves a lot of time during which you may seem to be getting nothing done. Not true. You are rethinking. Kafka hung a sign over his writing desk. It said WAIT.

30. The Emergence of Theme

During the rewriting process a new kind of discovery takes place. You begin to be aware of what your book is all about: the theme or themes imbedded in the people, place and action. Sometimes these themes come as a surprise. You may have thought you knew exactly what you were writing about, but if you let yourself go during the first draft, let things happen, you may have ended up using these events and characters to say something more, perhaps even something different from what you thought you were saying.

Flaubert said, "The word is never lacking when one possesses the idea." This statement could be interpreted to mean that the idea must come clearly first, to be then followed by the right word. But most of us, I suspect, move back and forth between word and idea, so that the attempt to find the right word—choosing, rejecting, rearranging—is the method by which we find and refine the idea.

When I wrote Ella Price's journal, I thought I was writing a bookabout education, about how a person's mind was opened and developed. During the first rewrite I realized that I had another theme aswell, the problems facing the learning person as a woman. During the fifth rewrite, two years later, I realized that my deeper under lying theme was the war between consciousness and unconscious ness, acted out in the struggle between Ella and her husband.

At each point of theme recognition I was able to do some things to strengthen the theme I saw emerging. This is ticklish business.You don't want to be hitting the reader over the head with a message. But every writer has a message whether or not he admits it oreven knows it. I think it's better to know it, to know as much as you can about what you're up to and, in the later stages of your re writing, to use your rational faculties to sharpen your point.

Whether or not readers consciously get the point, it is what gives wholeness to your novel. As Flaubert says, knowing what you're thinking is a wondrous help in finding the right words. It can be dangerous only if the "idea" you find in your story becomes a ruling despot, driving out everything but a propaganda slogan. But if you started with a "seed" and proceeded through intuitive first draft writing, you should now be able to heighten the emerging themes without letting them steamroller the life out of the book. It's merely a matter of sharpening a few words in a spot of dialogue, broadening a gesture, heightening an action.

That's what I tried to do when I rewrote and heightened the conflict between Ella Price and her husband Joe. Both Ella and Joe believe that Joe's easygoing expression of his character, "I'm happy if

I can eat, drink and screw," is a sign of his psychological strength. Ianthe first version Joe went on repeating this with no reaction from Ella. (I hoped the reader would catch on and get sick of it.) But in a late rewrite I added the scene where Joe says, for the umpteenth time, "I'm happy if I can eat, drink and screw," and Ella, to her own surprise, bursts out, "So is a pig!" This is her sudden realization that her discontent and questioning are signs of health, not neuroticism. It is also a statement of theme.

In Miss Ciardino every flashback memory that comes to Anna Giordano is a thematic statement. Her memory of Willie Fortuna states the corrupt administration afflicting many institutions. Her memory of Stephen states the special passion unique to the relation between teacher and student. And so on. As I worked and reworked these elements that went into forming her character, I was aiming toward some kind of assimilation of all of them. Not reconciliation to the injustice and pain she had suffered, but some way for her to assimilate her experiences and go through them to new awareness and a new life. I couldn't do it, couldn't find the right word or gesture that avoided psychological jargon or neat diagnosis or pat answers. Until a friend said to me, "You show how she's like her angry father, but you don't show any of her gentle mother in her. And it's that part of her that will heal her." I didn't agree with my friend (too pat) but her mention of the mother gave me an idea.

In a deathbed scene early in the book, Anna's mother sees visions of light and color. It occurred to me that in the final scene of the book, when Anna sees the new possibilities opening up to her, she might say something to show a parallel between her new vision and the vision of the "life beyond" which her mother had seen. So I changed the last lines, to show Anna looking at the fog breaking up, laughing, and seeing "... angel wings!" Then I changed the early deathbed scene, adding the angel wings to her dying mother's description of her visions. These two meaningless words made an emotional connection and strengthened my theme: that life can open up to great possibilities at any age, at any time.

Some writers say that you shouldn't think about theme. Whatever theme is there will just be there. Has to be. They're right, of course. You can see it in their work, a theme that runs through all their books, is part of their style, is what they are and what they have to say, as if each writer really has only one story to tell, over and over. So if you're superstitious about tampering with what your unconscious knows, or it makes you uncomfortable to think about theme, just keep tinkering, aiming to reach the surest, clearest effect of your story, and let them take care of itself. It's all the same.

31. When do you ask for criticism?

Some writers want their work read by others during all stages of its formation. I think this is all right for nonfiction writers, particularly if experts in the subject of the book can offer information. But I hold a strong conviction (call it prejudice if you like) that writing fiction must be individualistic, that we must resist the temptation to ask for help at every stage. (Unless you want, not criticism, but praise. In that case you can give it to a mama who pretends to reedit, tells you it's wonderful, and helps keep you going. Just don't confuse that with criticism.)

Sometimes I think that for at least the first five years you should write without showing anything to anyone. For a long, long time all you need to do is to keep on writing, and the only thing a good, honest critic could tell you would be how much more work you need to do. The best criticism in the world can't do you any good if you're not ready, not developed or strong enough to take it. It may just bowl you over, horrify you with the glimpse it gives you of how far you have to go. Even if you don't scare that easily, you may be hampered more seriously by the very help you get. Criticism, help, answers to writing questions may only defer the time when you finally, as Rile says, go deeply into yourself, to where the harder questions and the deeper answers are found.

This movement inward goes against our conditioning, which is designed, not to develop the broad potential of our talents, but to make us fit into society as it is. When everyone conforms, when the disruptions of artistic inspiration are suppressed, society runs smoothly, usually toward its own destruction. In the preface to *Saint Joan* Shaw states, more eloquently than I can, the inevitable clash between inspiration and authority. These days we are rarely threatened so directly as Joan was. Strong indoctrination toward dependency, through mass media and schools, enforces conformity more effectively than the threat of the stake.

We grow up believing that we must not believe in ourselves. If we want answers we must consult members of our group (family, friends) who are all busy consulting each other for the "right" answers. Sometimes we switch groups, and think the switch means we have learned to think independently; it doesn't. Or we consult "experts" and sometimes learn too late that they only represent currently entrenched interests and opinion, like doctors who prescribe a pill for twenty years before noticing that it causes cancer, if we want to do something, we look for a book or a class on how to do it, forgetting that one of the greatest American educators, John Dewey, insisted that we learn by doing.

What has all this to do with writing a novel? Everything. I know one good writer who, when she decided she wanted to write, had to sign up for a class before she could write a word. This was the only way she could think of to legitimize her decision, let alone put it into practice. Her greatest effort in learning to write had to go into weaning herself away from all the teaching and guidance she got, or into "squeezing the slave out" of herself, "drop by drop," as Chekhov once put it.

This may seem a strange statement coming from someone who taught writing classes for over twenty years. Am I now attacking them, biting the hand that fed me? Admitting it was all a fraud? Certainly not. A good writing class, taken at the right time, may be invaluable. What I am attacking is our tendency to be dependent on authority, opinion, consensus, help, the conditioning that made some of my younger writing students say in desperation, "Just tell me what you want!" and then go from desperation to angry disbelief when I replied that writing didn't work that way.

If you believe, as I do, that your function as a novelist is to be a voice for the deeper, unspoken dramas in other people's hearts, you are faced with a paradox: in order to speak most deeply for others, you must draw away from them. You must rely more and more on the solitary reaching toward your broader intuitive levels of consciousness. A further paradox is that while maintaining your independence, insisting on shaping your work according to what you alone see, you must also be humbly open to criticism and correction from outside. When you are ready.

Most beginning writers think they're ready before they really are. They and their work can suffer serious damage from premature criticism. Reading a partly written first draft of a novel to other people involves the critic too soon and may shatter your mood of play, cut off the stream of inspiration. This damage can be inflicted quite painlessly, as people give you enthusiastic suggestions. All the help would be just lovely, provided that good novels could be written by a committee. They can't. Remember Ogden Nash's definition of a camel: a horse made by a committee. In the case of writing, I'd reverse that image. Better to create your own funky old camel than a smooth little plastic horse designed by a committee of your friends, teachers, and relatives.

So my advice is, don't show your work to others until you just can't go any further on your own.

The sign that I am ready for an outside opinion is that I am suddenly overcome with disgust and an overwhelming desire to burn the damned thing. This desire usually comes during the third draft and means I need someone to take a fresh look at it.

32. Who should criticize your work?

The ideal critic is one who can see exactly what it is you are trying to do, better than you can, and offer suggestions on how to do it better. Henry James and Virginia Woolf exemplify this rare ideal. And it is rare. The most frequently committed sin of the best intentioned teacher, editor or reviewer is to read your book and then talk about how he or she would handle your material. You end up getting criticism on the book you didn't write and have no intention of writing.

Resign yourself to sorting through lots of irrelevant comments to find real, usable criticism.

Where can you get this criticism? From a group or an individual? A friend or a stranger? A writer or nonwriter? A professional or a "common reader?" Some writers could never even consider confronting more than one person with a piece of work, while others are energized by arguing with a crowd in full attack. Some live in large urban centers and have many options, while others live in rural isolation with hardly anyone to talk to.

All I can do for you is to list some possibilities and warn you about the dangers of each. Often, just being aware of dangers or disadvantages is enough; you can be on guard against the dangers while enjoying and using the benefits. In other cases, the disadvantages may be so damaging that you must avoid exposure entirely.

You will have to judge for yourself, according to your temperament and the choices open to you.

Let's take groups first.

The casual group of a few writer friends meeting in each other's home often suffers from its own lack of structure. Few ever manage to walk the thin line between flaccid acceptance of anything you write and vicious attacks which paralyze you. If such group doesn't break up from hard feelings, it may degenerate into asocial gathering, which may be lots of fun but a waste of time when what you're after is attentive, sharp criticism. Sometimes groups like this have a few good months before melting down, so you might try one for a while.

Some towns have open readings, that is, a group where people drop in and out volunteering to read. I've never gone to one. The thought of reading bits of my novel aloud to total strangers who may have dropped in for motives that have nothing to do with writing scares me more than walking down a dark alley in the roughest part of town. A man recently confirmed my fears by telling me he went to an open reading advertised in a student newspaper, stayed for a few horrified minutes listening to unleashed hostility, then made a quick escape. But another man told me he read for the first time to an open group where anonymity gave him courage and where his work was handled gently. Certainly an open group is a feasible starting point if you're a newly arrived stranger in town. You'll meet other writers, maybe one who can give you helpful criticism or leads to other resources. You can always go and sit, listen, size up the group. No one can force you to read if you don't feel comfortable.

What about writers' conferences? There you're in the open reading situation, but run by professional writers, often famous ones who might even take a fancy to your work and help get you published. That's the trouble. Many writers go to a conference hoping not for criticism but for publishing contacts. And just as many nonwriters go: agents, editors, teachers, would-be writers hoping for inspiration from the famous, and just people with faintly literary tastes, money, and time on their hands. The famous writers often go because an old friend who organized the conference invited them, so they can earn money while visiting with old cronies. This combination of motives can create a confusing atmosphere: for some writers a carnival of inspiration, for others a nightmare. Of the dozens of conferences advertised every summer, some, I am told, turn out to be "good," meaning the person who told me so came away feeling good. But I have seldom been told by a writer that she received direct, appropriate criticism on a long piece of work at a conference.

Wouldn't a class avoid all these disadvantages, offering a stable group with a teacher to control and guide criticism? Yes, but there are no perfect solutions; a class presents other problems. The teacher may not be adept at control; seeing to it that everyone gets sharp, useful criticism that doesn't demoralize and discourage them is a feat of orchestration. Classes usually operate on a schedule, often with assignments that don't fit the place where you are. Even if you are excused from the regular assignments, you may be called upon to submit part of the novel before it is ready. And turning in just a part of it also poses problems. In most classes there just isn't time for everyone (including the teacher) to read your whole novel. It's usually better to submit a short story and hope you pick up some general pointers that will help you with the novel.

Writing classes offered in a university with a high reputation tend to want to be as respectable as the academic disciplines surrounding them. So there's always the danger that a good class taught by good writer in a good college may start handing down rules for the construction of good fiction, according to what's orthodox at the moment. In a respected institution these prejudices carry weight. Istook my first writing class from a man who believed everyone should write like Hemingway. At the time, many teachers and students at that college agreed, and I was too ignorant to understand that the reaction to my work was influenced by that orthodoxy. I tried hard and did turn out some pieces that satisfied him. And it took a long, long time for my writing to recover from that success. By the way, this instructor was not a famous writer, but an insecure, underpaid graduate student, which is what you're likely to get in beginning class at a "good" college. Such a teacher can be very good or very bad depending on how she or he feels about earning a meager living this way while trying to write.

You might prefer an ongoing class or workshop in an adult school, outside of any degree program. Its value will depend on who's teaching it (word gets around when the teacher is good) and on who's taking it. The class may attract people for whom taking classes is a social function, a place to meet people. During my time I concluded that at least half the people in any class were there for motives having nothing to do with the subject offered. These motives are often social aims which tend to unravel critical aims, and it will be up to you to support the teacher in resisting the unraveling.

Sometimes classes contain people whose unraveling effect is subtle. They've read Henry James and E. M. Forster and all those interviews of famous writers. They know all the right things to say, like, "Show, don't tell!" And they can spot a point of view shift and shoot it down like the fastest draw in the west. Sometimes they're right, and you can learn a few things from them. But sometimes you learn that it's been a long time since they did any writing. They now are reduced to showing off what they know about writing, at your expense, and hence may be more destructive than the openly social types, who can at least be ignored.

The main benefits of a class are indirect. You get to talk about writing with people who take writing seriously whether or not they are really working at it. You discuss other people's writing problems and learn some general things to apply to your own writing. A good class, taken at the right time for you, can give you standards for writing and plenty of information. It can save you time, getting you through some early mistakes faster. It can be a very important form of publication, supplying an audience to spur you on during the probably many years before you get anything in print. It can balance the loneliness of your solitary, silent hours of writing.

But the best class in the world still has one danger: it can become habit-forming. When I was still teaching, serious writers signed up for my classes again and again. Of course, I felt flattered, but then I began to wonder if I was having a bad effect on them. I was supplying pressure for them to write, supplying instant criticism of writing hot off the typewriter, supplying a place for them to go when they were stuck, struggling, uncertain.

What's bad about that? Well, I'm not sure you should always get outside help when you're stuck. Maybe, as Rilke tells us, that's when you have to sink deeper into your solitude, into depths you didn't know were there. Maybe you have to go through these depths and come out the other side. Remember the story of the child who saw the moth struggling to get out of the chrysalis? Wanting to help, he took his knife and cut the chrysalis open, and the moth, its strength not developed by struggle, fell to the ground unable to fly.

After getting what groups can offer, the serious writer usually begins to look for one person who will read the whole novel and react to it. Who should that person be? Again, I'm going to issue warnings, then let you choose from whoever is available to you.

Showing your work to friends or relatives can be a weird experience. People who are close to us have a certain view of us which may exclude other views. They may be unable to take you, their friend or wife or brother-in-law, seriously as a writer. They may have a deep resistance to your writing at all. They may be jealous of the attention you give to writing. They may be afraid of finding themselves portrayed in your novel, or disappointed at not finding themselves in it. They probably can't divorce you from your book, and their image of you may always get between them and an objective reading.

Even if your friend or relative is sympathetic and fairly objective about you as writer, she may lack the qualifications to give you the help you need. A friend who never reads anything but gardening books may be of little help with your novel (though he may surprise you). Even more dangerous can be your cousin who is getting her PhD in English Literature. The young academic steeped in Shakespeare and Milton may try to prove her impeccable taste by measuring your book against impossibly high standards.

What about another writer? Someone you met in a class or work shop or conference. You could exchange manuscripts and help each other. This sounds like an ideal solution, but somehow it's harder than it ought to be to form a couple or trio of writers who like each other and each other's work. I have often found that I love talking about writing, agreeing on general aims and problems, with a writer whose work bores me and whose attitude toward my work infuriates me. Perhaps writers are especially prone to the sin of imposing their own will on another writer's material.

What about paying someone to criticize your work? This has the advantage of making you think twice, revise again, do all you can independently before shelling out hard cash. But you should be very careful. Remember, millions of people cherish a secret wish to see their words in print. Exploiting this desire is big business. You are a candidate for the longest sucker list in this country. In order to stay off that sucker list, you must follow one firm rule: pay money only to recognized, accredited schools (colleges, universities, adult schools) or to individuals recommended by qualified people you know.

The safest way to spend your money is to pay for a college or adult school extension course which offers criticism by a teacher editor you never see. You send in your work, and it comes back to you with written comments and suggestions. Wherever you live, even on the most remote island, you are within reach of one of these programs. Write to state supported colleges or accredited private colleges until you find one with such a program. You can't be sure of getting the ideal critic, but you can be sure your critic has some recognized qualifications to do the work, will charge a fair price, and won't pressure you into signing a long term, expensive contract (a sure sign of a crooked operation).

Another fairly safe way is to hire a freelance editor by the hour to read your work and offer criticism. Remember the rule: hire only one recommended by someone you know. If you ask around, you can get good advice from a teacher or another writer. Try the person they recommend. Within a short time (after a few hours pay) you should be able to tell whether or not this editor is helping you. If not, scout around for another, and keep hiring and firing until you get the help you need.

Despite all these warnings you should be able to find a group or individual to give you the feedback you need. You'll just have to try, make your mistakes, and keep trying to pick up good criticism wherever you can. As your needs change, you'll probably have to keep searching for new kinds of help.

I went through many dismal, useless and harrowing experiences before I found my friend Betty, who is widely read enough to be tolerant, a writer (in a different field) who knows how hard writing is, a woman with long experience as a librarian and an editor. In addition to these qualifications, she is without envy, ego or prejudice when she looks at a manuscript. She likes me and my work generally, but is not afraid to speak up strongly against what she doesn't like. I don't always agree with her, but I respect her judgment, and I know I can trust her to want my work to be the best / can do.

After a general reaction from Betty, I test the manuscript on people with specialized knowledge: on medical or legal people if a scene contains something pertaining to their specialty, on a lesbian, on an actor, on an adolescent, anyone who can fill me in where distance or inexperience may have tripped up my imagination.

95

Whoever reads and criticizes your manuscript, there is one unbreakable rule: type a clean, proofread copy for your reader. If you don't respect your work enough to present it in good form, you shouldn't expect anyone else to. And keep a copy; things do get lost.

33. How should you take criticism?

The truth is that you don't want to know what is wrong with your novel. You're tired. You want to be done with it. You deserve praise just for working so hard. All you want is to be told that the book is wonderful; therefore you are wonderful. You feel, not that you are submitting a manuscript for criticism, but that you are submitting, exposing yourself. And in a way you are.

Usually the first reaction you will feel toward criticism will be anger. You will feel you are being attacked and must fight back. In some cases you may be right, and the so-called criticism is really an attack. It's hard to tell. I have learned not to trust my first response. I can't be sure of the value of criticism while I am hearing it. Like the first draft of the book, it has to cool first.

The best way to take criticism is just to take it all in, making notes, asking questions to make sure you understand exactly what the critic is saying. Make no reaction at all, no matter what is going on inside of you. Put the criticisms away in your head, send them to your subconscious. Sleep on them. Mull them over for a few days, even weeks, before you decide whether or not you can use them.

Sometimes the criticism that made you most angry turns out Tobe the most useful, and you were angry because you knew, deep inside, that accepting the criticism means a lot more hard work on the book. My friend Betty says that she always recognizes good criticism by her instant, furious realization, "I knew that part was weak, but dammit, I hoped I could get away with it!"

Sometimes, after thinking it over for a couple of weeks, you'll decide that the criticism you received was careless, stupid, prejudiced, hostile and completely beside the point. In other words, it is not useful to you and may be ignored. Try to see all criticism that way, simply as useful or not useful. Let it cool, examine it. Use it or discard it. Don't bother to get angry and defend yourself (either directly or in those long, furious monologues that keep you awake all night) against a critic who didn't understand and can't help.

You save a lot of energy that way. And you save healthy anger for real battles.

34. Read it aloud.

Sometimes when I do a public reading, someone will come up to me afterward and say, "I've read that book, but this is the first time I've heard it read aloud, and you know, it sounds good." The personas surprised and looks as if she thinks I must be surprised. I'm not, because I read the book aloud five or six times before it was printed.

You may have read parts of your book to people at various times for criticism, but now try a different kind of reading, a reading of the whole book, daily, in one hour sessions, to someone whose major qualification is the love and patience to put up with hearing it over and over.

After overhauling and criticism, before typing the next clean version of the manuscript, I read the whole book aloud to my husband, who just listens and reacts spontaneously. Often he doesn't have to say a word. I can sense when he's bored, or see his frown when something isn't clear or his eyelid flick of surprise when something doesn't fit.

But more important I can tell, by the sound of my own voice, how the words fit together. How they feel in my mouth, how they sound, how sentence follows sentence, how words lead to other words... and when they don't. When I read aloud I hear errors that never caught my eye. Yet, this won't work if I try it alone. I need a listener.

Try it, and I think you'll find it essential. Just remember that you're not doing a public reading; don't read too well. Don't dramatize and add emphasis. Read in a quiet, expressive voice, but not too expressive. Make the words do the work as they must when they are read silently on the printed page.

Sometimes I can get my husband to read aloud to me. Or my children. Any average-to-good reader over the age of twelve should be able to read your work aloud without stumbling. If he does stumble, you probably need to reword that part.

Reading aloud is very good for spotting repetition. I do some of my best cutting during a reading aloud session, and good cutting is one of the most important parts of rewriting.

After reading aloud, I'm ready to go back through all the parts of the cycle of rewriting until I get, finally, a reading aloud that sounds, if not perfect, not changeable.

35. When is it done?

How many times must you go through the cycle: letting the manuscript rest, reading it through, making changes, getting outside criticism, reading aloud?

Gogol said a manuscript had to go through eight such cycles, eight perfectly clean versions, done by the author's own hand, rewritten to the point of illegibility, then recopied and torn apart again. Balzac and Hemingway drove printers crazy by doing more revisions on galleys. Flaubert worked over Madame Bovary for seven years. Joyce worked on Finnegan's Wake for seventeen. Henry James, near the end of his life, revised most of his early novels for a new edition of them.

It has been said that no book is ever really finished; it is simply abandoned.

When is it time to abandon it? That depends on the book. There comes a time when I feel so removed from a book, so different person from the one who began it, that I can see no point in doing anything more to it. This feeling may come after only the second rewrite, as it did with *Kin of Ata,* which was done within a year, including rest periods. But more often I think I have abandoned it, only to look at it two years later and then be able to see what it needs, as I did with Ella Price's Journal. I revised Miss Giordano five times over a period of six years. After each revision I felt certain I was done with it forever. I have had one huge novel in my file for almost ten years. Every couple of years I take it out and work on it again, then put it away. Someday, when my writing strength has grown to match the demands of that book, I'll finish it.

There is always the danger of too much rewriting. Tolstoy said that sometimes he changed wording just because he was bored with phrase, substituting something worse than the original. And many readers prefer the earlier versions of James' novels. Too much revision can take the life out of a book.

There comes a time when a book should be abandoned because it's about as good as it can be. Randall Jarrell once defined a novel as a story of some length "that has something wrong with it." That "something wrong" may just be built into the book, intrinsic to the story and the form it had to take. Flawed as the book may be, it's time to quit.

Besides, one of those card boxes is filling up. A vague but intriguing set of characters surrounds you and is beginning to close in. The faint but growing excitement is sweeping away the mood of dust drudgery in which you typed the final, final version. You are starting to believe that writing could become fun again. You are ready to start your next novel.